Devotions to Refresh You in Your Work

Proverbs for Busy Women

Edited by Mary C. Busha

Contributors include Normajean Hinders, Peg Rankin, and Nancy Pannell

Nashville, Tennessee

Printed in the United States of America

4253-88
0-8054-5388-1

Dewey Decimal Classification: 242.643
Subject Heading: Devotional Literature \ Woman—Religious Life \
Bible. O.T. Proverbs
Library of Congress Card Catalog Number: 94-36448

Interior design by Leslie Joslin
Cover design by The Puckett Group

Library of Congress Cataloging-in-Publication Data

Proverbs for busy women / Mary Busha, editor.
p. cm.
Contents: 1. Devotions to refresh you in your work — 2. Devotions to build up your relationships — 3. Devotions to strengthen your walk with God.
ISBN 0-8054-5388-1
1. Bible. O.T. Proverbs—Meditations. 2. Women—Prayer-books and devotions—English. 3. Christian life. I. Bushā, Mary Catherine, 1945–.
BS1465.4.P76 1995
242'.643—dc20 94-36448
CIP

This book in the series
is dedicated
to my sweet children
who made up the
homes in which I have
lived and worked.

I have not always exemplified
the productive and excellent woman
described in Proverbs 31,
but I have loved the Lord
with all my heart, soul, and mind.

I pray that love is
what you will carry with you
into your own homes and places of work.

I love you!

❧

Acknowledgments

Mary C. Busha

A special thanks to all of the women who allowed their work to be shared on the pages of this book. They've opened up their hearts and lives in their writing. I know their experiences will be used to minister to many women in their homes and workplaces. It has already ministered to me over and over as I have worked to compile and edit this edition.

A special thanks, too, to Janis Whipple, editor at Broadman & Holman, for believing in this project and to Broadman & Holman Publishers for allowing this dream to continue.

On a personal note, I want to thank my husband, Bob, for his special kind of love and encouragement.

Contents

Introduction

Wherever we call our workplace, whether in the home or out, or both, we have many challenges before us: to achieve balance in our workday, to be sensitive and caring to those around us, and to be content in knowing that we are, indeed, accomplishing that which the Lord has set before us. Added to these challenges are the many church, school, and community activities in which we feel compelled to take part.

Never before have women had as many labor- and time-saving devices. Never before have we been given as many choices as to how we will spend our time. And, yet, we're still frazzled and worn out.

The writers who have contributed to this volume understand, because we are there! We, too, are trying to achieve some semblance of balance in our routines for living. We, too, are often worn to a frazzle.

But we have a source of strength, our precious Lord God who in His Word has given us encouragement and counsel. We invite you to share in our experiences and in the wisdom contained in the Book of Proverbs as it pertains to today's busy woman in her home and work.

Committed to His Work

Gloria Anderson

Commit your work to the Lord,
and your plans will be established.
Proverbs 16:3, RSV

When Bible reading and prayer were banned from the public schools, I wondered how I, as a teacher, could help children realize how important these elements are in their lives.

In a neighboring city, a teacher continued the practice of reading the Bible to his students and he was fired. Protesting his demise left him without a teaching position. "What good did it do for him to protest?" I asked myself. No one rallied behind him. How sad.

When I went into teaching, I committed my work to the Lord. It seemed unreal, however, that our government, which had been formed on Christian principles, had ruled any form of religion out of the public schools. I wondered how it would be possible under the circumstances to fulfill my commitment.

"Lord," I prayed, "show me how I can share Your love with my students when such a law exists."

The first fifteen minutes in the morning that had formerly been devoted to Bible reading, prayer, and reciting the Pledge of Allegiance became a time of inspirational readings, after which we would stand to salute the flag and bow our heads for a moment of reflection. I told the students that I liked to say a prayer to start the day and suggested that maybe during that moment of silence they would like to say one too. After that, our scheduled classes would begin.

One day one of my students asked if she could talk to me right after school. When all of the other children had left, Cindy came over and said, "Mrs. Anderson, would you pray for my grandma? She's awfully sick." It was then that I knew God had answered my prayer to Him about my commitment. In spite of the circumstances, He was still in control.

Only God knows how much Christian influence I had on the young lives of the students I taught. My assurance was that as long as He was at the center of my plans, my work would be blessed. And it proved true during all the years I taught in the public schools.

Dear Lord, I commit my work to You. May Your plans and my plans always be the same. Thank You for always being there for me. Amen.

Worship, A Strong Tower

Linda Atterbury

The name of the LORD *is a strong tower;*
the righteous runs into it and is safe.

Proverbs 18:10, NASB

I love to sing, especially worship songs to the Lord. Fast, slow, soft, loud, meditative, or foot-stomping, it really doesn't matter as long as His name is being lifted up.

One afternoon my four-year-old and I were boisterously singing old Maranatha praise songs. We were clapping, raising our hands, and doing a variety of movements, when suddenly it struck me how free and uninhibited we were. We had forgotten ourselves completely. Neither of us worried if we were too loud, undignified, off key, uncoordinated, or out of rhythm. We were having fun praising the Lord! We were giving our full selves unreservedly to worshiping God and raising up His name. Our hearts were open and our true faces, unmasked, were upraised to Him. Because His name was

being lifted up, we felt safe and secure in His strong tower. Praising Him released such joy in us and bonded us that much closer together.

As we finished our medley, there was a tug at my heart. Was I always so free when worshiping God? Did I not often draw in, tone down, monitor, and dilute my praise, especially when worshiping with adults? And in those moments was I not taking my eyes off of the Lord and letting self creep back in? Had I not allowed insecurity, the need for acceptance and approval from others, and self-consciousness to steal my freedom and rob me, and those with whom I was worshiping, of the fullness of joy and strength of unity that praising His name in worship brings? Yes, I had stopped resting in that safe, secure tower and had thrust myself back into the fearful uncertainty of the world.

It took singing with that sweet, open four-year-old, who had no sense of self when worshiping God's name, to open my eyes. How humble I felt. Yet how gently God redirected me toward His safe, strong tower once again.

Lord, thank You that Your name is worthy of my praise. Help me always to keep my eyes toward You and daily to take refuge in Your safe, strong tower.
Amen.

3 Our Cluttered Stable

Mary Jane Behm

An empty stable stays clean—but there is no income from an empty stable.
Proverbs 14:4, TLB

Our neighbor down the street invited me in for a chat one day. Everything in her home was in place: the coffee table with a perfect floral arrangement set carefully on its polished surface; the sofa with each cushion in place; the chairs sitting primly. There was no dust, no clutter. Suddenly I realized there were also no books, no magazines, no newspapers. And there were no touches that gave hints that she or her family had lovingly created something—a needlepoint pillow, cross-stitch picture, crocheted doily, or handmade rug.

Then I heard my friend ask, "What on earth do you do now that you and your husband are retired?" People often ask that question, perhaps just making polite conversation, but this lady was sincerely asking, almost with a tone of desperation in her voice.

"I get so bored," she said. "Television gets tiresome. My husband and I find ourselves running out of things to talk about. We were used to lots of people around at the office. We don't know what to do with ourselves now."

I couldn't help feeling sorry for her. Yet when I suddenly pictured our all-too-cluttered house, with books and magazines overflowing their shelves, a cross-stitch pillow in process, notebooks and pens within easy reach, typewriter and computer ready to go, and possibly some of my husband's tools in a corner where he parked them momentarily between projects . . . well, I had to stifle a sudden urge to laugh!

I complain sometimes because our calendar gets too crowded with volunteer activities, writing projects to complete, letters to answer, telephone calls to make, or household chores to be done. My fretting isn't about how to entertain ourselves but about how to keep ahead of the clutter.

Certainly, my husband and I are never bored or wondering what to do. Our mutual interests and projects provide ample topics for conversation. Our activities help us to form new friendships. And hopefully we are able to fulfill needs in the lives of others.

I thought again about the verse from Proverbs. No, our stable is not empty. It doesn't stay clean. But the "income" is marvelous!

Lord, thank You for our cluttered stable and for all that makes our busy lives possible. Amen.

Restraining the Wind

Jan Boatwright

A constant dripping on a day of steady rain and a contentious woman are alike; he who would restrain her restrains the wind.
Proverbs 27:15–16, NASB

A somber, gray sheet covered the sky as tiny flecks of cold, sleety rain pelted the bookstore. Standing at the window, I watched the puddles outside growing. "Let me see just one tiny hole of blue sky, one little ray of sunshine," I grumbled. "I can't bear one more gray day!"

It was springtime in North Idaho, and a battle raged within me. I wished I could run away, but I had nowhere to run and no way to get there. My trapped soul screamed as I turned back to the dusty shelves always needing attention.

The little bell on the door announced my visitor before I heard his cheery voice sing out, "Nice day, isn't it?" I turned and saw a man in a battered, yellow rain slicker. His bare head protruded from the coat as water dripped from his dark, plas-

tered hair to his unkempt beard. Outside the door the bicycle he had been riding stood propped.

Before I had time to tell him how truly horrid I thought the day, he grinned and said, "I've been out catching worms." When I realized he was serious, my mouth fell open.

"I'll put them in the gardens," he continued. "This year I'll help the Smiths with their garden, and the Bordens." The light on his face reflected the summer harvests he already envisioned.

He was not an angel, but a real flesh and blood man who visited our store often. For him, life was a simple matter of loving God, sharing the gospel of Jesus Christ, and helping others; consequently, catching worms was as important as witnessing to the governor of our state, which he had also done.

My own discontent stormed, at war with this man's peace. Even though I was warm, dry, and surrounded by the Christian books I loved, I complained. Yet he happily picked worms in the cold, sleety rain. His simple joy finally disarmed me and conquered my strife-ridden soul.

Contention is difficult to restrain, and yet nothing is too difficult for God. He sent this gentle soul to restrain the winds of my discontent.

Jesus, thank You for loving me when I am not lovable. You are not contentious; instead You are meek, gentle, and humble.
Amen.

Rescue Work

Elisabeth Buddington

Rescue those being led away to death; hold back those staggering toward slaughter.

Proverbs 24:11, NIV

I was tired of my volunteer work with Birthright. I was sick of going into the office, bored with the meetings, frustrated with the complex and unending problems of the young girls and women who came to us.

"Should I take a leave of absence or resign?" I asked myself. After all, of the thousands of babies being aborted every year, was the handful I was involved in bringing to birth really significant? And I certainly could use the extra free time if I were no longer committed to this.

The phone rang in the middle of my considerations. It was Jane (not her real name). Jane, whose calls came in regularly and always presented me with a challenge. Jane, who had no living parents, no friends or relatives nearby, and who found in this middle-aged woman someone to whom she could talk.

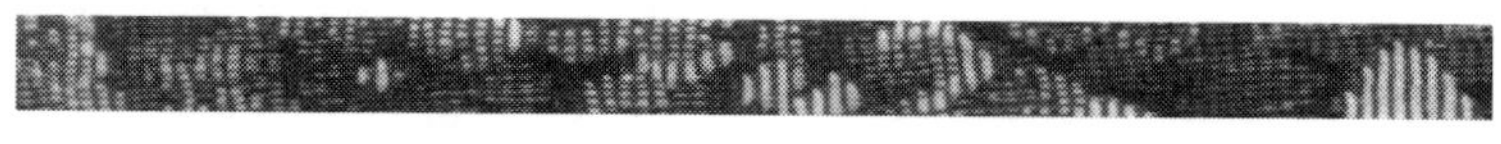

A new problem had come up, and she asked my advice. (Never mind that she rarely took it!) She updated me on the progress of her first baby, the one through whom we had met. Jane had been homeless and alone, and I had helped her receive housing and medical care. Then she asked what I would do in regard to the problem with the second baby. We chatted awhile and then the call was over.

I sat staring at the phone. From somewhere deep inside a smile formed and made its way to my face. I wondered if the Lord sometimes feels as I did—weary of trying, frustrated by the irresponsibility of His people, annoyed when they don't try His simple ways of dealing with life's difficulties. Somehow, through this rescue work in which I was involved, I was seeing a tiny bit of what He goes through in His major rescue, that of saving people for an eternity with Him.

No, I concluded. He is too big and too holy to be limited by any human type of frustration. His goal is too momentous and dear to His heart to want to give up. And if my desire is to be His woman doing His work in my tiny sphere, I had better ask Him for the means to continue.

That was it. That was my answer. To keep trying, just as He does.

Lord, rescue work can be grubby and strenuous and frustrating. Help me to see beyond this to Your ultimate purpose and help me to keep on keeping on.
Amen.

My Love Affair with Words

Mary C. Busha

Train up a child in the way he should go, and when he is old he will not depart from it.
Proverbs 22:6, RSV

My love affair with words began several years ago as a little girl, when I sat nestled beside my father on the living room sofa watching attentively while he worked the crossword puzzle in the evening newspaper. From time to time he'd even ask my advice, as if a five-year-old had much to offer in the way of the English vocabulary. But with enough hints on his part, I'd guess a few words right.

In addition, Daddy was a speech-maker. On a few momentous occasions he would invite me along to his weekly labor union meetings, and from the audience I would shoot admiring glances at the podium where he so eloquently voiced his concerns for his fellow workers. Of course, I didn't understand much of what he was saying, but I was so proud.

In preparation for his speeches, Daddy literally read the dictionary, jotting down those words he was not familiar with so that he could go over them again and again. To include me in the process, he would mark those unfamiliar words with a little dot beside each one and then have me make a listing in a little spiral notebook he carried around in his shirt pocket for easy reference.

In school, English was always one of my favorite subjects, from spelling bees in the elementary grades to term papers in later years. When I was a child, I enjoyed reading everything from my grandmother's worn Bible to my mother's recipe books to comic books and Nancy Drew mysteries. Today I work with words: writing, editing, and producing books.

Daddy's not around any longer; cancer took him at an early age. But I think he'd be proud of his daughter. I know he'd enjoy seeing some of the fruit of his labors. When he didn't even know what he was doing, he was training up his child in the way she should go, and she hasn't departed from it since.

Dear heavenly Father, thank You for my earthly father who loved words. Thank You, too, that he loved his little girl enough to let me work closely with him when neither of us had any idea of the plans You had for me as a woman. I love You, Lord, and I loved him dearly.
Amen.

MORE PRECIOUS THAN RUBIES?

Suzanne P. Campbell

When she speaks, her words are wise, and kindness is the rule for everything she says.
Proverbs 31:26, TLB

Reading what Proverbs has to say about women has always depressed me. Who is this mythical beast who gets up before dawn, holds the distaff and grasps the spindle with her fingers, while opening her arms to the poor and extending those same hands to the needy? All this, while she is planting a vineyard, clothing her family in scarlet, making coverings for her bed, and selling her homespun linen so she can buy a field? She may be more precious than rubies, but she just sounds tired to me.

One day I came upon Proverbs 31:26 about kind speech. It sounded like someone I could be. It's kind to look at a child's drawing of a green and yellow blob and say, "Tell me about it," rather than, "What on earth is that?" My husband and I

always did this when our children were small. A teenager's new hair-do can be greeted with guffaws or respect for his attempt at taking charge of his own personhood. Liking the new "do" isn't the issue, loving him is.

I've been on the receiving end of this kindness too. One Sunday, dinner stayed in the oven too long. After cracking open the meat loaf with powerful knife blows, my husband served. "Honey," he said later with a hug, "The meat loaf we scraped from the center tasted great." My meat loaf may have been a failure but I wasn't, and how wonderful that feels.

I don't advocate false flattery, or pretending all is well when it isn't. I do believe that kind words are an option I don't choose often enough, and I intend to work on that, especially since a recent incident. My seventeen-year-old daughter teaches the two- and three-year-old Sunday School class at church. I watched as one of her students ran up to her in the narthex with a drawing done in cheerful colors but totally unrecognizable. "How wonderful, Brittany," she said. "Tell me about it."

Lord God, I can't be a perfect woman, but I can choose to be a better one. Help kindness to be the rule in all my speech. Help me to know I am more precious than rubies to You, and I don't even have to compete for the title. Amen.

Jerking Heads and Wagging Fingers

Rosemary Lemcool Capen

If you search for good you will find God's favor; if you search for evil you will find his curse.
Proverbs 11:27, TLB

My heart sank one morning as I stepped off the elevator. I could see two coworkers talking at the nurses' station. I didn't need to hear them. Their jerking heads and wagging fingers spoke all too clearly; their round of complaints had already begun. These criticisms sounded the same every day: their assignments were unfair, no one else did enough work, nor did it right; their husbands slighted them; their kids were rotten; patients were demanding and ungrateful; merchandise was shoddy and prices too high.

Their stream of grievances battered my ears for eight hours. Their habit seemed so ingrained that the two of them knew no other way to converse.

I was concerned, though, not so much about their problem as I was my own. For I'd found, when listening to them, I'd

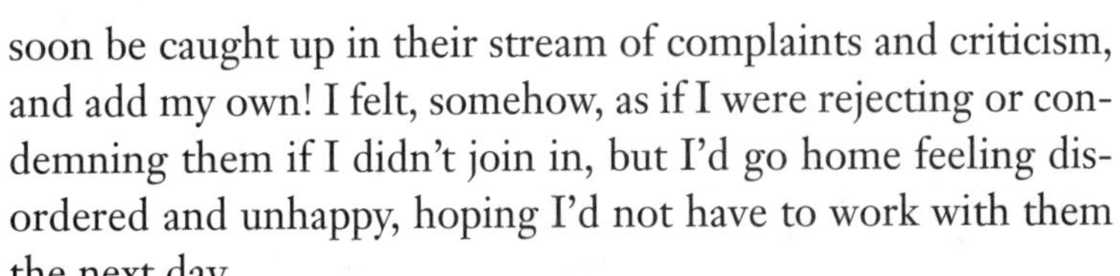

soon be caught up in their stream of complaints and criticism, and add my own! I felt, somehow, as if I were rejecting or condemning them if I didn't join in, but I'd go home feeling disordered and unhappy, hoping I'd not have to work with them the next day.

One morning while preparing for work, my devotions included Proverbs 11:27. *How true*, I thought. *Continually talking negatively leaves me feeling as though I'm living under a curse*.

I determined to search for good and enjoy God's favor. As soon as I reached work, I said something complimentary to each of the two complainers about their work or their appearance. Then I kept quiet, evicting from my mind any negative comments that crept in. I searched for positive thoughts during the day, voicing them when it seemed appropriate.

My positive outlook didn't change my coworkers. They continued relating tales of mistreatment and the inadequacy of others, but I didn't join in. I remained determined to search for good and find God's favor. Daily I felt exhausted, but blessed, as I headed for home.

Precious Father, help me to remember always to look for the good in every person and situation. May I remember to seek Your blessing, shunning the curses that follow a negative attitude.
Amen.

Quiet Wisdom

Lynn Casale

When words are many, sin is not absent, but he who holds his tongue is wise.
Proverbs 10:19, NIV

Slam! went the car door as my daughter climbed in after school. "It's my turn to sit in front. Can't you remember anything?" she snarled at her sister. "And move your stupid backpack!"

"Here we go again," I sighed to myself. I had tried many ways of dealing with these after-school outbursts, but nothing seemed to be working, and I didn't know what to do.

I confessed as much to a friend who taught school. She told me about a system she used in which she handed out a tally for misbehavior and a certain number of tallies would result in predetermined consequences. I thought it was worth a try.

I turned to the Scriptures for some wisdom and came across Proverbs 10:19: "He who holds his tongue is wise." I designed some tally cards with those words printed around a large cartoon mouth.

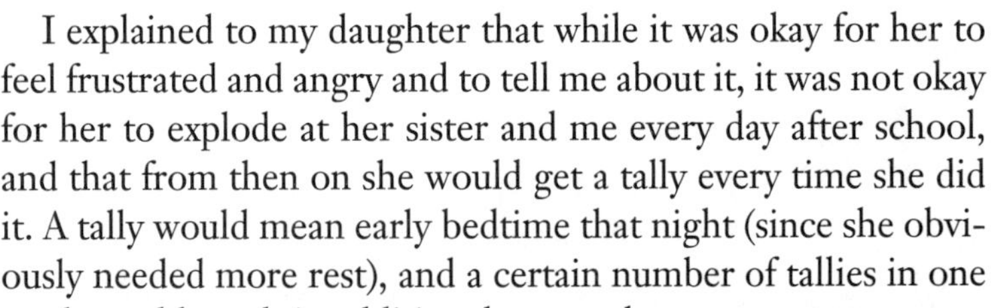

I explained to my daughter that while it was okay for her to feel frustrated and angry and to tell me about it, it was not okay for her to explode at her sister and me every day after school, and that from then on she would get a tally every time she did it. A tally would mean early bedtime that night (since she obviously needed more rest), and a certain number of tallies in one week would result in additional unpopular consequences.

The system worked well. My daughter learned to give herself a time out if she felt an explosion coming, in order to avoid the dreaded early bedtime. I handed out a few tallies, but after a month or two we didn't need the system anymore.

But the lesson didn't end there. God had something for me to learn as well. While my daughter was discovering that it helped to talk directly to me about her frustrations, I was rediscovering the importance of listening actively and holding my tongue. I needed to give my daughter an attentive ear and a quiet mouth that refrained from jumping in with advice or admonition as she shared her feelings. Then I needed to repeat back to her her own words. This helped her to feel heard, and that's what she had wanted and needed all along.

Set a guard over my mouth, O Lord; keep watch over the door of my lips. Help me to be quick to listen and slow to speak. Make my restraint a loving gift to someone today. Amen.

Tending Flocks

Alicia Chai

Be thou diligent to know the state of thy flocks, and look well to thy herds.
Proverbs 27:23, KJV

Listening to my uncle talk about his many missionary journeys, I couldn't help but become a little envious. For it had been the desire of my heart since childhood to do exactly what he had done, to travel the world spreading the gospel of Jesus Christ.

Being naive, I always thought that it would be not only a fascinating occupation but one full of wonder and excitement. So I spent much of my time planning and dreaming of the places I would go and the people I would see in the darkest regions of the earth.

As I continued to listen to my uncle, I began to doubt if being a wife and mother were important at all. Were they really as worthwhile as being a well-known evangelist? Had I missed my calling? Perhaps I should be somewhere telling

thousands about Christ and leading them though the prayer for salvation. How could doing laundry, cleaning house, or wiping a child's runny nose ever compare to such accomplishments?

However, I have grown in my understanding. I have come to realize that it is foolish to compare my accomplishments with those of others. For we are not all meant to be evangelists, pastors, or prophets.

Our tasks are as varied as the results of those tasks. God only demands that we be obedient to that which we are called to do. God's perfect will for me may be in doing what someone else would not.

I have learned that real accomplishment is not always in the seeing of mighty results but in knowing that the task was performed well and with an obedient heart.

I still feel my heart surge when my uncle comes to visit. His stories cause my mind to wonder what it would be like to be in Africa, Asia, and other countries of the world. But I have learned that I can listen without feeling despondent. For as long as I am doing God's perfect will for me I am in a good place.

Now I spend my time praying for the missionaries across this world and taking joy in the things God has called me to do. I have made sure that my own flock is well tended and that they are raised as unto the Lord.

Dear Lord, help me to be faithful and diligent to those things You have called me to do. Let me not be discouraged with unseen results but encouraged because You take joy in obedience. Amen.

King of the Mountain

Pauline Ellis Cramer

When a king sits on his throne to judge, he winnows out all evil with his eyes.
Proverbs 20:8, NIV

During recess duty I watched my second-grade boys play king of the mountain. This gave me an idea. When the children returned to the classroom, I asked them what they would do if they really were a king or queen. Their answers ranged from "Kill all the bad guys" to "Make people be nice to each other." This led to a discussion of what they would do if they were king or queen of our classroom. My final questions were "What if the only person you could rule was yourself? What would you command yourself to do?"

"I'd command myself to make all A's!" one tiny girl answered.

"I'd command myself not to talk so much and not to get in trouble," one boy blurted out without raising his hand.

Then another girl tentatively raised her hand and asked, "What would you command yourself to do, Mrs. Cramer?"

Taken by surprise I stammered, "I . . . I guess I would command myself to be the best teacher possible."

Later that day I thought about that question. Unlike King David or Solomon, I'm not responsible for ruling a worldly kingdom, but I am responsible for governing my inner kingdom of thoughts, feelings, and decisions. God has given me free will to decide to submit my internal kingdom to His edicts. I am responsible for keeping the lines of communication open between us.

I had to ask myself: Do I allow Christ to be King of my heart? Do I give Him permission to winnow out the evils of pride, envy, hypocrisy, a critical spirit, or an irritable disposition? Am I reluctant to allow Christ to winnow away the chaff of my sins, and then do I blame Him for the lack of joy in my inner kingdom?

Today I will truly be the queen of my own kingdom with Christ as my King. I give thanks for the wisdom, patience, and peace that comes to my world when I command myself to emulate the life and teachings of my King.

Dear God, I praise You for the discipline and comfort You bring to my inner kingdom. Amen.

Your Plans Established

Eugenie Daniels

Commit thy works unto the Lord, *and thy thoughts shall be established.*

Proverbs 16:3, KJV

Sometimes we can't see how something we feel the need to do can be accomplished. That was how I felt when I read about the famine in Africa and saw the horrible pictures of starving people. What could I, one homemaker, do to help?

It was just after Thanksgiving in 1984 that I went to the checkbook to send what money we could afford; I was only able to scrape together seventeen dollars.

Later that day I went to the kitchen to make an apple pie for the church supper that night. My pies are quite popular, so I'm always asked to bring one. Then the idea came to me. Why not use the seventeen dollars to buy ingredients and have a pie sale to raise more money for those starving people?

I had a basket of apples my sister had given to me, which would help. I decided to try it.

Then I began to ask: How would I make all of those pies? Where would I hold a one-woman pie sale in the beginning of December? Would people in our small town buy the pies or would I come home with too many pies to put in the freezer and no money to send to the hungry?

I prayed, "Lord, I want to help the people in Africa. I am giving this pie sale to You. Please help it to succeed."

First, a friend volunteered to help. Second, I got the idea to hold the sale on a Saturday morning on the busy corner by the bank. The church gave me a table and the bank agreed to let me set up outside. The Lord was working for me; Saturday was sunny and not too cold.

I felt funny standing on a busy street corner in my heavy coat behind a table holding fifteen apple pies. Although I had a sign to say what the sale was for and a can for the money, nothing happened for the first half hour, which was very discouraging.

However, the Lord had established my plans; three hours later all of my pies were gone. Some people had even contributed extra money. On Monday morning I sent off a check for $140 to help the starving people of Africa.

It's good to know that even when we cannot see how our work can be successful, if we commit what we're doing to the Lord, He will establish it for us.

Dear Lord, I want to bring my work before You and ask that You establish my thoughts and plans for Your glory.
Amen.

Fondue for Dinner

Kimberly De Jong

In his heart a man plans his course, but the LORD determines his steps.

Proverbs 16:9, NIV

I plan my family's dinner menu weeks in advance. If I see an idea in a magazine or a family member has a special request, I write it on my menu calendar.

My daughter had been requesting her favorite dinner, fondue, for several months. Our financial situation, however, had hit a low. Fondue is one of the most expensive dinners I prepare. I told her, "Soon, we'll have fondue, I promise." In my heart I wanted to grant her request, yet my brain told me it was too costly.

After repeated pleas from my daughter, I finally put fondue on the calendar for a month in the future. I was confident our financial situation would improve by then and I could treat my family to fondue.

Weeks passed, and as I prepared my grocery list I noticed fondue was in the week's menu plan. Our financial situation had not improved; it had become more strained. How could I tell my daughter, again, that we couldn't afford it? After all, I had promised her. But steak and shrimp were too costly.

I decided not to worry. Worrying wouldn't change our financial situation or her desire to have fondue. I put my problem in God's hands. I knew He would provide an answer.

Later that evening my husband came into the room to tell me he had found six steaks in the bottom of the freezer. Six overlooked steaks from earlier months of more abundant money. Six steaks which would now become two meals for my family—two unexpected meals.

The savings on those two meals would cover an inexpensive cut of steak and a small amount of shrimp for fondue. If I added the leftover chicken breasts in the freezer and some fresh vegetables, we would have a feast. My daughter would have her fondue after all. Thank You, God, for little miracles.

Dear Father, thank You for all the little answers to prayer that confirm You care about me. Thank You for the struggles I face, because through them I grow closer to You. Amen.

THE LAST SPANKING

Mary Jane Donaldson

Discipline your son in his early years while there is hope. If you don't you will ruin his life.
Proverbs 19:18, TLB

"Mom, do you remember the last spanking you gave me?" my son, John, asked one night while he and his wife, Dena, were visiting.

"How could I forget?" I replied as my memory traveled back in time to a particular evening in my son's life. His adolescent, teen years had been a lot of fun, but they had also been laced with rebellion, turmoil, strife, and the battle of the wills.

My husband, Johnny, and I believed in spanking as a last resort, but there were a few offenses that brought an automatic spanking the first time. One of them was sassing your elders, especially your parents. John had a way of testing that rule to the limit, and one night he went too far. He left me no choice but to make him pay the consequences of his actions.

Now, years later, he is a policeman, enforcing laws and dealing daily with rebellion in every form.

"Mom, the other night I received a call concerning a twelve-year-old boy. I took him home, and when we arrived his mother told me that her son was out of control and for me to take him somewhere else. It made me furious. I stared at her and asked, 'Ma'am, you're telling me that you have a twelve-year-old you can't control! Who's the boss here?'

"She stared back at me with the most discouraged, defeated look in her eyes and said, 'He won't listen to me. He says his life is his own and he'll do whatever he wants with it. You should hear the way he talks to me! I can't take it anymore. I have younger children to think about. Officer, what am I supposed to do?'

"For a moment I didn't know what to say, then I remembered how I was when I was young. 'Ma'am, I, too, was a rebellious teenager. Let me tell you what my mom did to me once when I sassed her.'"

I laughingly commented, "Now, you're telling me you're thankful for that night."

"You bet I am," he replied, smiling down at me.

Tears splashed down my cheeks as I looked into the eyes of my son, now a man. Silently I thanked God for His Word that teaches and guides and works in our lives.

Lord, thank You for the awesome privilege of being a mom. I praise You for redeeming what at the time seemed so difficult to handle and for giving me the wisdom years ago to discipline my son early in his life.
Amen.

Better Days Ahead

June Eaton

Do not boast about tomorrow, for you do not know what a day may bring forth.
Proverbs 27:1, NIV

My teaching career had come to a screeching halt. Married late, with three children under three, I dragged myself through each long day, unable to keep up with the never-ending demands of motherhood.

"I handled classes of thirty youngsters at a time," I wailed. "Why can't I manage three babies without becoming angry and frustrated?"

"Better days ahead, Mother," my husband would say every time my frustration level reached a new peak. Soon self-pity set in and I was fast headed for martyrdom.

"I can't wait until these kids are all out of diapers," I'd complain. Or, "Why can't she feed herself without making such a mess!" Or, "If only she were potty-trained." I kept wishing away each day in favor of some unknown tomorrow.

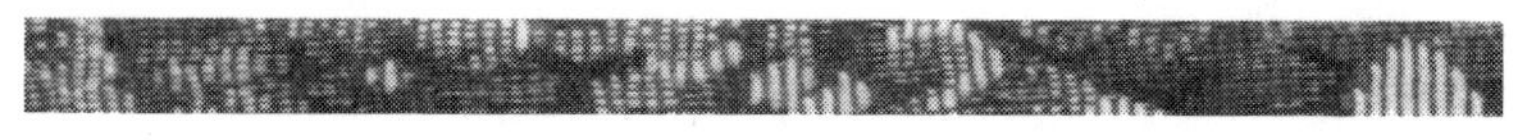

At each outburst, my husband would dutifully pat my shoulder and utter his comforting phrase, "Better days ahead."

Then one day a tearful neighbor appeared at the door, seeking advice about her school-aged child, a reluctant reader. Her level of worry and frustration surpassed my own.

"She's come through all of this," I reasoned after she was gone, "and things don't seem to be any better for her. She's not any happier than I am."

The next time my husband opened his mouth to utter his now-famous bromide, I stopped him mid-phrase. "Wait a minute," I argued. "Something's wrong with that philosophy. It's not tomorrow we should be concerned with. God has given us today to enjoy. He wants us to be happy now."

"You're right," my husband agreed. "We don't know what will happen tomorrow. Our 'better days' are right now!"

We looked into our girls' faces and knew we'd discovered a profound truth. That simple change in outlook made a big difference in my life. I resolved to search for the beauty of the moment, to find joy and humor in even the simplest acts of today instead of wishing our lives away. I learned to joke about the messy diapers, the walls painted with gooey cereal, and the endless mountains of laundry. My reward was a growing sense of happiness and contentment with the most important career of my life, caring for our three precious daughters.

Lord, help me continue to savor the joy
of each new day until I reach the tomorrow
of eternity with You.
Amen.

A Spider's Hands

Susan M. Ezard

The spider taketh hold with her hands,
and is in kings' palaces.
Proverbs 30:28, KJV

The spiders in my kitchen are tucked away in hidden corners where people usually can't see. On occasion a friend will spy one of them and shudder. I will then explain how a little insect taught me a great lesson.

"How can I count for God?" I lamented one day. "All I ever do is cook and clean and play taxi!" I also worked full-time to help my husband with household expenses. This didn't leave much time for a "special" ministry, and I often felt as though I just didn't count for God. When I heard a missionary talk about adventures on foreign fields or listened to musicians perform sweet, melodious numbers, I wondered how on earth could I ever be as worthy as they?

As I opened the window that day to let the fresh, clean, autumn air into our home, something caught my eye. In the

bushes by the side of the house was a brand new spider web. It stretched out in the early morning sun like a delicate bridal veil. Droplets of dew sparkled like diamonds, and for a moment I was mesmerized by its simple beauty. I knew that the web hadn't been there yesterday, and I marveled at the talent of that spider. How wonderful, how almost magical! God had given that tiny creature the power to create a thing of great beauty. All she had to do was perform the task that God had put before her.

As I admired the web, I wondered about my own talent. I shared a strong, loving marriage with my husband, and my children were happy. My employer was pleased with my job performance, and I had many friends that added a special dimension to my life. Then I realized that God had given me the same special blessing as the spider. I only need faithfully to perform the task that God has set before me and I will also create a thing of great beauty, something that will adorn the King's palace for eternity.

Father, help me never to grow weary of the task You've set before me, no matter how great or small.
Amen.

Honeycomb Words

Nancy Simmons Ferguson

Pleasant words are as a honeycomb, sweet to the mind and healing to the body.
Proverbs 16:24, AMP

"Mom, where are my shoes?" cries Megan. "Are we having cereal for breakfast again?" complains Patrick. "Why don't you give me enough time to get ready for school?" whines Hayley. "Honey, do I have any shirts to wear?" calls Bob, my husband. "Have you seen my briefcase?"

Too many questions in the morning bring out the grumpies in me. I feel like asking a few things myself. Like of my children, "Do your shoes have legs?" "Would you like to fix breakfast yourself?" "Didn't I call you the first time one hour ago?" Or of my husband, "Are your shirts usually in the closet?" "Am I your briefcase's keeper?"

Lashing back was second nature for me. For too long, I vented my anger in the mornings as my loved ones frantically

searched like hungry, blind mice in a maze for homework, shoes, briefcases, and car keys. When everyone left for the morning, it was with tears or in anger. And I wondered why they were in such a bad mood!

Later I noticed that my mood seemed to set the tone for the rest of the family. When my emotions changed, theirs did too. It amazed me.

As an experiment, I prayerfully and patiently helped my family find lost articles. Miraculously, they stopped complaining. I discovered that hugs did more to calm flare-ups between children than discipline. Cooperation improved as I wooed them into happy frames of mind.

Today, when my husband comes to breakfast, I kiss him good morning. "You look handsome today," is sure to straighten his shoulders and send him out the door with a smile.

"I'll be praying for your big test," I call to my nine-year-old as she leaves for the bus. She runs back to hug me.

"You did a good job making your bed," I say to my three-year-old. With a big grin, he puts a few toys back on his shelf.

Words have power. Pleasant words produce pleasant results. It feels nice to send my family off to face the world with a few loving and encouraging words. And sometimes . . . I get pleasant words too. "You're the best mommy in the whole world!" "I can't wait to come home to you after work!"

Dear Father, guard my tongue from thoughtless remarks. Let my words be acceptable to You and let them help build up my family and others. Amen.

Angry Words

Nita Walker Frazier

*A quick-tempered man does foolish things,
and a crafty man is hated.*
Proverbs 14:17, NIV

Just as a quick-tempered man does foolish things, so does a quick-tempered mother. I rushed around the house, throwing a load of clothes in the washer, setting out a roast to thaw, brushing my daughter's hair.

"Mom," my son whined. "I need . . . "

"You have everything you need!" I snapped. "Do you have your books?"

He nodded. "But I want you to check my homework." His words didn't register. My only thought was to hurry, hurry, hurry.

Finally, I herded the kids out the door, both armed with coats, backpacks, and lunch money. My son carried an extra burden, a deep frown.

"Mom," he said timidly, three blocks from home, "I left my homework on the table. Can we go back and get it?"

"Homework is your responsibility," I yelled, "not mine!" You'll get a zero today because we can't go back home. If we go back, we'll be late for work and school. Why did you take your homework out of your backpack in the first place?"

With each word I got louder and angrier. My son, I reasoned, had to learn to shoulder his share of responsibility.

His small face clouded. "Beslowtoanger," he mumbled, running his words together. Then louder, "Be slow to anger."

"What?" I asked. I was the teacher here, not this eight-year-old who used a memory verse to quell my mounting anger.

"I left it because I wanted you to check my work before I turned it in," he said, bravely trying to conquer the tremor in his voice. "I was afraid I'd get a bad grade if you didn't check it."

He was worried about a bad grade, which could affect his yearly average. I was worried that I wouldn't be the first one through the office door.

Why was I so angry over such a little thing? Would being ten minutes late cost me my job or only my pride? What of my son's pride in his homework papers?

My answer to my son's request that I retrieve and check his homework accomplished nothing, which is precisely why God tells us to be slow to become angry. Anger stands in the way of the people He wants us to be.

Father, teach me to count to ten so
that the person You want me to be, not
the anger, speaks.
Amen.

SECOND CHANCE

Linda Gilden

Anyone willing to be corrected is on the pathway to life. Anyone refusing has lost his chance.
Proverbs 10:17, TLB

This morning as I was teaching my class of five-year-olds, they were having a particularly hard time paying attention. Some chatted with their neighbors, and others shouted messages to friends across the room. Justin and Mallory were still talking as I began to give instructions for the songs we were going to sing.

"Justin," I said, "I'm afraid you and Mallory will have to sit for five minutes in the gym. When you use your time in class to talk, you'll have to give up some of your playtime."

Justin's face fell to his chin, and he looked at his shoes. His drooping shoulders said more than words. I felt my soft spot surface.

"Okay," I said, "we'll let that be a warning. But please show me for the rest of the session that you know the right way to behave during music."

He looked over to Mallory and broke into a big grin as he vigorously nodded his head. One big tear escaped as he silently thanked me for a second chance.

Right then I had to quietly thank my heavenly Father for the many times He's given me a second chance. In my heart I want to always do and say what is pleasing to God, but often I fall short of that goal. I don't get around to reading my Bible one day, another I speak unkindly to my family, or another I miss an opportunity to minister in word or deed just because I am too busy or too tired. But God loves me so much that He gives me another chance to do these things. Sometimes He even has to give me more than a second chance. Sometimes it takes a third or fourth. How thankful I am for His love and patience with me!

Dear Lord, thank You for Your patience with me. Make me willing this day to accept Your love and correction in every area of my life. Amen.

The Togetherness of Retirement

Carol Green

Trust in the* Lord *with all your heart and lean not on your own understanding.

Proverbs 3:5, NIV

"Lean not on your own understanding." These words circled slowly in my mind like a dog readying his place to sleep at night. I smiled. Why these words now, Lord? Wasn't this, my husband's retirement, a phase, another passage in our marriage? Wouldn't we get through it like we had all the others—the skinned knees of childhood, the challenges of the teen years, the uncertainties of sending our three off into the world, and praying about their prospective mates?

Somehow I know my favorite saying, "This too shall pass," wouldn't work for the foreverness of retirement. Now my husband was always there, for breakfast, lunch, and dinner. His lunch at 11:30 sharp. Mine, whenever I finished the morning tasks. And coffee breaks? What are those?

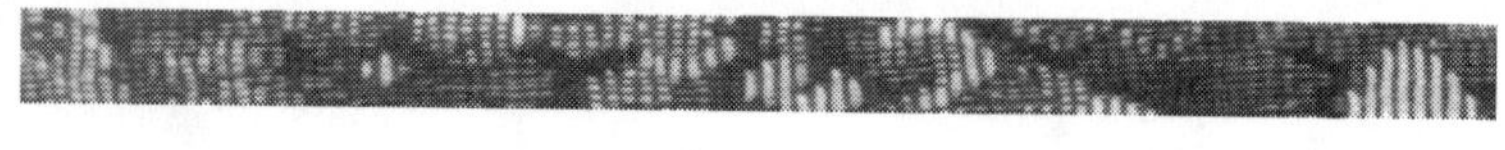

Lord, how can I understand all of this; what is my place, my space? All those years of his place at work and mine in the home. Now he's a presence heard but not always seen, puttering in the yard and in the garage, opening and closing the refrigerator door. How can I write, even do the laundry?

"Trust Me," the Lord seemed to whisper. "Trust Me."

I stood up from my quiet time humming a gospel tune I had not thought of in a long time, "Leaning, leaning, leaning on the everlasting arms . . ."

I called out the window to my putterer, "Want a glass of orange juice?" I could take a few more minutes to relax. *Lord, am I beginning to lean on Your understanding, not mine?*

My husband set down his finished glass of orange juice and with a hearty aaah, said, "Isn't this great! No schedules, no phone calls. Just this . . ." He watched a hawk soar on the wind.

I laughed to myself.

Lord, help me not to trust my own wits, but to lean on You, to smooth the wrinkles of finding our space, our place in this, the togetherness of retirement. Thank You, Lord, that I have You to lean on and not myself.
Amen.

On God's Payroll

April Hamelink

The fear of man brings a snare, but he who trusts in the LORD will be exalted.

Proverbs 29:25, NASB

My husband and I mingled at his company picnic. As a mother at home, I felt out of touch with fashions and adults in general, and was more than a little nervous. But I was beginning to enjoy this party. I was meeting many of my husband's coworkers, people I had heard lots about but had never met. Then it happened. Someone asked the dreaded question.

"April, what do you do?"

How I hate that question. Too many times I stammer out something like "Oh, I'm just a mom." Red-faced and embarrassed, I then retreat someplace to hide. Don't get me wrong, I love what I do. I wouldn't trade peanut butter and jelly kisses for a desk and paycheck any day. My greatest joy is to feel two chubby little arms around my neck and to watch the unre-

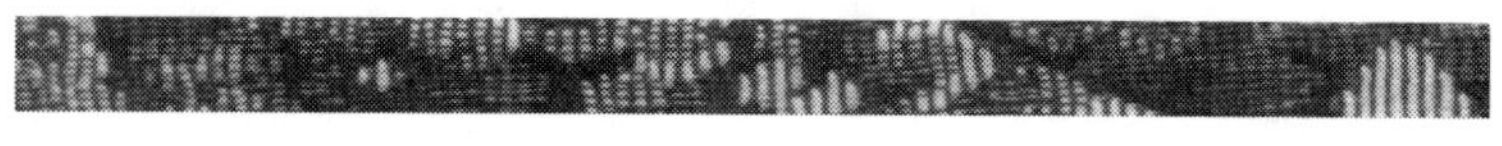

strained joy of my children. I feel very privileged to be able to stay at home.

Why do I hate this question so much? Because of the response I usually get. People often give me an indulgent smile and say things like "Aren't you lucky" or "I'd go nuts if I had to stay home all day" or "Don't you get bored?" Then they turn away as if I could have nothing to contribute to any conversation and ignore me for the rest of the evening. Women's roles are so varied today. We have so many choices. Yet it often seems the roles most valued are the ones for which you receive monetary payment.

Behind me I heard a voice come to my rescue. "She's the best wife and mother anybody could ask for!" I shot my husband a grateful look as he continued to sing my praises. As I listened, I saw myself through new eyes.

I realized that the fear of what others would think was a snare to me—a trap that led to doubt and a poor self-image. By staying at home, I was right where God wanted me, and if I would only trust Him, He would exalt me in His way, in the eyes of my husband and children.

I no longer mumble that I'm just a mom. Rather, I hold my head high, look people right in the eye, and tell them that I'm privileged to be able to stay at home and be with my children. God has truly given me an exalted place.

Father, thank You for the privilege of serving You at home. Help me to trust You and to be grateful for the place in which You've placed me.
Amen.

A Wise Message from My Daughter

Normajean Hinders

The reproofs of discipline are the way of life.
Proverbs 6:23, RSV

My twenty-one-year-old daughter Gretchen and I spoke recently about the transition she is in and how she views herself.

She spent last year studying art history in Italy. Upon returning she hoped to apply and enter the university system at the winter quarter. Due to financial cutbacks, however, winter admissions were closed. As a result, she could not return to school for a year.

She spoke of this summer season in this way: "I feel very comfortable and confident with the choices I've made this year. At the same time I'm definitely out of sync with my peers. I'm working, but not toward a career. I'm not connected with academics, which have defined my purpose for

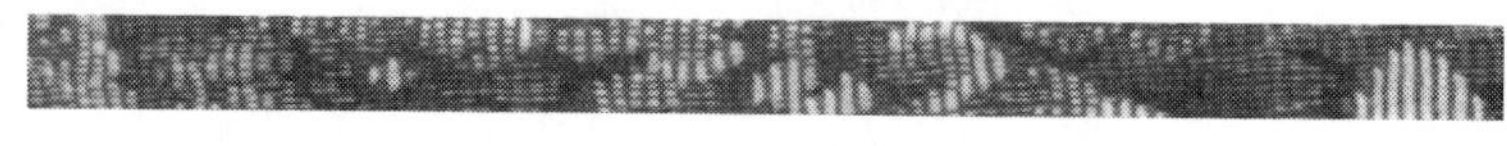

years, and I'm not readily part of a group. I guess I'm experiencing sadness and joy both at the same time. Not being in school makes me very sad and sometimes depressed. On the other hand, I really know I can be and do anything I set my mind to.

"I could be an excellent pianist or graphic designer if I wanted to. I also know I've accomplished things that make me feel very good about myself. I'm self-assured in my abilities, and I like the way I'm handling the year of waiting—at least I'm not stagnating. I know I'm in a good place when I enjoy what I'm doing *as I'm doing it,* that I feel what I do is worthwhile and that I am making a difference. You know what it feels like? It feels like I'm floating in warm ocean waters—settled, contented."

I loved the emphasis she gave to how she did what she did. She enjoys her tasks and commitments as she is doing them. She allows herself to be nurtured by what she chooses.

Heavenly Father, thank You for those wise words from my daughter. Help me to remember that whether at home or at work I'm in a good place when I enjoy what I'm doing as I'm doing it!
Amen.

QUALIFIED FOR MINISTRY

Marion R. Hocking

She looks well to the ways of her household, and does not eat the bread of idleness.
Proverbs 31:27, RSV

I qualified easily for the "Virtuous Woman of the Year" as depicted in Proverbs 31. The never-ending carousel of chores had me dizzy.

By default I had inherited two preschool grandchildren. While I loved them dearly, increasingly I did not love what came with them—Tinker Toys, mountains of laundry, and endless interruptions.

Certain that God had led me to take a leave from teaching to care for these two adorable waifs, now it was getting to me. I wanted time to read about something other than Bugs Bunny. I wanted time to write. Most of all, I wanted to be through with children at 3:00 P.M. sharp so I could spend a quiet evening with my husband.

One night, engulfed by self-pity, I journaled in ever-increasing-sized letters, *I hate housework!* Seven times I wrote it, complaining loudly on paper.

That was when I heard His still, small voice, which impelled me to keep writing, "For the Son of man also came not to be served but to serve, and to give his life" (Mark 10:45). The insistent voice continued, "A servant is not greater than his master" (John 13:16).

Ouch! The ears of my heart got the message. This is my ministry. This is how I am to give my life—washing mountains of little jeans and piles of dirty dishes, cooking endless meals, settling frequent "he-hit-me-first" quarrels.

Oh, Lord, I wrote, *I am your servant. And You have given me this ministry. Help me to accept it cheerfully.*

In the days that followed, I accepted anew the challenge of servanthood. Always busy? For sure! Looking after my family's needs? To the best of my ability, including failures and successes.

I felt deeply rewarded one afternoon. In the backseat of our car, four-year-old Jennifer was singing to herself, "Jesus loves me, this I know, 'cause the Hockings told me so." That's when I decided there is no greater honor or privilege than to be Christ's servant in my home.

Thank You, Lord, for the ministry of looking after my family's needs. Help me to be a busy and faithful servant, willing to give my life for others and for You.
Amen.

Camera-Ready

Jo Huddleston

Above all else, guard your heart, for it is the wellspring of life.
Proverbs 4:23, NIV

My eyes serve me like a camera, clicking away on an endless roll of film. Each evening my mind develops the snapshots, and I discover my day's mood stamped across them.

On stressful days, it's obvious my impatience has spread intimidation across my sweet child's face. Pictures taken on difficult days reveal a loving husband, now reserved, letting me pour out my frustrations on him simply because he's there.

Images from these warped days unveil store clerks, bag boys, and even neighbors, perplexed at how to handle me. They withdraw from my nearness, uneasiness lining their faces.

My mind's screen displays people whom I hurt this day. Oh, I didn't bring them physical pain or even verbally insult them,

but my attitude quenched their happiness like water splashed on a campfire.

Confronted by my camera's disclosures, I declare my shame before God. Sleep overtakes me as I seek God's forgiveness for not being His approved witness today.

After such an imperfect day, I awake the next morning asking God to cleanse my heart, knowing it's the wellspring of life. Scripture reminds me diligence is necessary in the housekeeping of my heart, because what starts from within will affect every aspect of my life. It's essential for me to search my heart and clear out dust balls of negative thoughts—to replace them with wholesome thinking on things which are true, noble, right, pure, lovely, and admirable.

Maybe today I'll see my child's bright eyes that, yesterday, clouds of my impatience darkened. Today I'll speak more kindly to my husband and see his relief as I hold my tongue. Perhaps my smile today will signal store clerks, bag boys, and neighbors they don't have to cross to the other side of the street when they see me coming.

Tonight, before I surrender to sleep, I'll thank God for loving me no matter what my mood. God knows and tests my heart. His unconditional love can equip me to meet every day. God's joy can make me camera-ready so that my daily pictures will please Him.

Dear God, I don't want to hurt anyone today.
Please help me maintain a clean heart and an
attitude pleasing to You.
Amen.

Too Much Stuff!

Judy Hyndman

Better is a little with the fear of the LORD, *than great treasure and turmoil with it.*

Proverbs 15:16, NASB

Slowly I opened the door to our large walk-in closet and sighed. What had started out as neatly packed boxes filled with favorite books, photographs, and clothing had ended up a miscellaneous mishmash. It had all been tossed in together during those final hours before our departure to New Zealand. I was hoping the mess would have disappeared in the year we'd been gone.

I don't remember having this much stuff! Didn't I already sort through this craft bag? Why did I keep an entire box of college term papers? An outdated leather coat, extra shoes, hats and shirts . . . this is relying on the Lord?

Overwhelmed, I plopped down in the nearest chair, my stomach tied in knots like a child who'd had too much candy.

Why am I having such turmoil sifting through the treasures I used to call "old friends"?

Lord, what treasure is it that I long for, that we captured during our sabbatical? There were those many predawn moments of thanksgiving and prayer when I sat on our living room sofa with a steaming mug of tea. I continually praised You for the soft golden hues of the sun rising on a gentle sea and the brilliant green backdrop of the countryside.

Yet even more enticing than the beauty and serenity of the country itself was the retreat to simplicity, the Lord reminded me. A small, simply furnished home, tight budget, fewer choices, and less to organize allowed us many blessings: extra family time, more quiet moments to reflect on His daily provisions, and fresh energy to carry out the few goals He had set before us.

I looked closely at some of those valuables in the closet that took a lot of my time, things that had to be cleaned, fixed, arranged, or shelved. Was it overindulgence that caused the turmoil? Were my possessions opposing the simple lifestyle the Lord wanted me to live?

Eliminate and concentrate, I vowed with new vitality. I began to fill up the Goodwill box. As I hesitated over a spare jacket, the Lord gently nudged me, "Pass on some of this stuff and focus on the treasures that will last an eternity."

Lord, help me to remember that all this stuff will burn someday. But the treasured times I spend in Your will last forever.
Amen.

The Kiss of Truth

Rosalie B. Icenhower

An honest answer is like a kiss on the lips.
Proverbs 24:26, NIV

One day a mother regaled me with the capabilities and intelligence of her five-year-old son and requested his placement in first grade.

"What do you think?" she asked. "Is that a good idea?"

Sometimes it's difficult for me to give a straight answer. It's not so much that I don't know the answer as it is that I am reluctant to bruise a mother's pride.

With the experienced eye of an educator, I could see several warning signs of immaturity. The slightly built child was climbing restlessly in and out of his chair, clinging to his mother, and sucking his thumb. I knew it could be disastrous to place him in a classroom full of six- and seven-year-olds who were at least a head taller and quite obviously more

mature than he, so I tried to talk her out of the placement without expressing my opinion.

I explained the school's admission policy: First graders were to be six years old by August 31. The persistent mother argued that every rule has an exception. I asked if she would be willing to have the child tested by a psychologist to assess his maturity level. She protested that the testing would be neither acceptable nor necessary and that they could not afford the additional expense of having such an assessment.

Finally, I blurted out, "If he were my child, I'd wait until next fall. He needs another year to be just a little boy."

Much to my surprise, she suddenly nodded in agreement. She told me that she had been pressured by her in-laws to ask for the bypass of usual admission regulations. She and her husband had given in, though they themselves were unconvinced of the wisdom of advanced placement.

"I was waiting to hear your opinion, since all four of us respect you and agreed to abide by your personal judgment. We didn't want to know about the school's policy or have psychological testing for our son. We only wanted to know how you honestly felt," she said.

My truthful answer had been like a kiss of affection to the concerned parents, and it settled all agitation from the grandparents.

Father, let Your truth be like a kiss on my lips today. I don't need others' rules nearly as much as I need Your honest appraisal of my weaknesses and immature walk with You. Amen.

Gentle Response

Sharon Lessman

A gentle answer turns away wrath,
but a harsh word stirs up anger.
Proverbs 15:1, NASB

"I hate you, I hate you! I'm going to rip your new watch off and break it!" screamed Sandy, inches from my face. Trembling inside, I continued reading a recipe with Betsy and replied softly, "I love you, Sandy. You know, I really love you a lot."

Soon Sandy stormed into her bedroom, still muttering under her breath about how much she disliked me. I breathed a prayer of relief and thanks to God that His word from the Book of Proverbs had proven true in my life.

Several years ago I worked as a program director with adult women who were mentally handicapped. One of the residents, Sandy, had a history of being physically violent, to the point of hurting others. After several incidents occurred at her apart-

ment and her place of work, each staff member was asked to formulate ideas to deal with the problem.

One of my suggestions was to try responding to Sandy with a soft, calm voice, instead of with angry, harsh words charged with negative emotion. Although the program was not Christian-based, the other staff members accepted this suggestion as valid. Through this and other ideas we were able to respond better to Sandy with love and patience.

We all encounter many situations in which our first reaction is to strike back and allow sharp, painful words to rush out of our mouths. But in these situations, whether with our children, spouses, fellow workers, store clerks, or others, God would have us respond with a gentle answer full of love.

Of course this is not always easy to do. It was very difficult for me in the situation with Sandy to remain calm, loving, and focused on Jesus. To respond in love with kindness and patience requires prayer, practice, and reliance upon the Holy Spirit's prompting in our hearts.

Using gentle words allows God's love to be a present reality in our circumstances. A soft, kind answer can diffuse anger, as it did with Sandy. It can also bring order and peace into a chaotic situation. A gentle answer does, indeed, turn away wrath.

Faithful Lord, thank You that Your Word is true and that the guidelines You have given me for living really do work. Remind me that in all I say and do, by the power of Your Holy Spirit, I can respond with gentle answers, full of Your love.
Amen.

Brick by Brick

Leslie McLeod

The wise woman builds her house, but with her own hands the foolish one tears hers down.
Proverbs 14:1, NIV

My toddler has collapsed, half on, half off the sofa, sleeping at last through a stuffed nose. In his crib, the baby struggles in a fitful tug-of-war between rest and waking. With my husband away this weekend, I'm a ping-pong ball caught between a voracious newborn and a sadly deposed two-year-old hanging on to Mommy like a bad case of static cling. Last night's dinner is cemented to the dishes in the sink, and the laundry frowns at me from its ominous tower in the closet. I haven't accomplished a thing in two days.

Or have I?

I've rocked and read, diapered and disciplined, sung and sworn to be the best mother I can. I've laid one more very important brick in the foundation of my children's lives and

prayed for the Lord to build those precious edifices strong and sure.

I know a woman who also remained home to raise her children, yet without seeking the Lord's gracious intervention. Locked in a world of calculating self-absorption, she gradually destroyed her relationship with her husband and with each of her four children. Adults now, one fears her, another hates her, a third uses her, and the fourth merely pities her.

Building a home with the help of the Carpenter or tearing it apart brick by brick through self-interest and neglect; there, and only there, lies the difference between wisdom and folly.

Lord, I possess no inherent wisdom. Apart from You, I feel completely inadequate for the tremendous task of raising my family. How grateful I am that I can count on You to supply the wisdom I need.
Amen.

No House for Barbie and Ken

Joyce Magnin-Moccero

Rich and poor have this common:
The Lord *is the Maker of them all.*
Proverbs 22:2, NIV

My four-year-old daughter looked up from the pink, plastic Barbie Corvette she was pushing.

"Mama?" she asked with taffy sweet sincerity. "I'd like to have a Barbie house so Barbie and Ken can have a place to live. Can you buy me one?"

"Not now," I answered in my best mommy voice. "They're too expensive. Maybe we can make one out of a cardboard box and some construction paper."

The crocodile tears began to pour in torrents. "But, Mama, I just have to have one," she pleaded. "I wish I had a rich mommy who could buy me everything I want."

With that, Rebekah stormed out of the living room and up the stairs. Then SLAM! In a matter of seconds she was in her room sobbing because I couldn't afford a house for Barbie.

I looked down at the abandoned car. Barbie and Ken sat in plastic perfection oblivious to the scene that had just unfolded. *They seem pretty content to me*, I thought.

But my daughter wasn't. She wanted to give her dolls the best. She wanted a rich mommy. I started to feel that my husband and I had failed.

Just then Rebekah tiptoed into the room. "It's okay, Mommy," she said, wiping her runny nose on her sleeve. "I still love you. You don't have to be rich."

I stretched open arms to my little girl. "Oh, but I am rich," I said. "Maybe I don't have a lot of money. But I have you and little Emily and Daddy. And I have Jesus living with me."

Rebekah went back to pushing the pink Corvette. "Mama?" she asked after a few minutes. "Does Jesus live with rich people too?"

"Of course," I chuckled. "After all, it doesn't matter if you're rich or not so rich. God made us all, and God loves us all the same. And no matter how much money we have, Jesus will move right in and live with us forever, if we ask Him to."

Lord, thank You for Your Son, Jesus Christ.
Thank You for the riches You've given me.
Help me to be content with Your provisions.
Amen.

MEDIUM-SIZED PROBLEMS

Gina Halford Merritt

The crucible for silver and the furnace for gold, but the LORD *tests the heart.*

Proverbs 17:3, NIV

When we built our new house, we expected perfection—no more apartment complex; instead, peace and quiet and a yard for the kids to play in. We'd be able to coast along for years without major repairs too.

Not long after moving, however, we found out that our house wasn't perfect. There were annoyances: crucial outlets had been omitted by the electrician; the back porch light blinked on and off; and when it came time to wash windows, they were not nearly as user-friendly as the salesman had predicted.

Now, four years later, our quiet street has been discovered by other new residents. Traffic has increased. Hot-rodders barrel over the hill in front of our house so often that I can't let our little children play in the front yard. The trouble is, they

can't play in the backyard either! The backyard has drainage trouble and often turns into a sea of mud. Now we just paid a landscaper to correct the problem, but it's almost as bad now as it ever was, and the landscaper doesn't seem to care.

We aren't rich. The landscaping fee represents months of savings. Our plan was to fix the yard first and then fence it to protect the kids from traffic.

While reading my Bible today, I worried about the mucky yard. Finally, in spite of my spiritual dullness, I realized that maybe God was trying to teach me something through all of this—like to trust in Him, get my eyes back on Him, and get my priorities right.

The yard isn't a small problem. I'd rather lock the keys in the car, have the washing machine break, and have my two-year-old fling spaghetti onto the front of my best blouse—all on the same day.

But it's not a big problem either. A friend of mine just lost her husband after a two-year battle with brain cancer. She knows about big problems.

My mucky backyard will not make me like the heroes of the faith mentioned in the Book of Hebrews, nor cause me to partake in the fellowship of Christ's sufferings. I'm afraid it's not a furnace for refining gold.

But maybe, if I yield to Him, it can be a crucible from which God can bring forth some silver.

Lord, please help me to keep my eyes on You,
to be grateful to You, and to remember the
things that really matter, instead of becoming
so mired in fleeting, earthly problems.
Amen.

A FEAST OF MORSELS

Barbara A. Micek

Better is a dry morsel with quietness than a house full of feasting (on offered sacrifices) with strife.
Proverbs 17:1, AMP

My shoes pinched, my head throbbed, and my energy level was sinking fast. I had just stepped into the house from a normally stressful day at the office, and my family was already in need of my time, attention, and care.

My six-year-old was eager to share her excitement of winning the school writing contest, while my ten-year-old needed an understanding ear to vent her frustrations of the day. My two teenagers needed a ride to their after-school jobs, and adding to the frustration was a loaded laundry hamper ready to burst, plus last night's spaghetti dishes, which no one's schedule permitted time to tackle.

I began to deliberate, *Is the second income worth it?* I studied the frustration on my family's faces, as well as the hopeless circles of stress I felt mentally.

Although Proverbs 17:1 was continually whispering to my spirit, I reasoned, *How can the bills get paid without my working?*

It wasn't until the mental pressure became almost unbearable, and massive chest pains warned of a second chest pain attack, that I made the decision to seek God's will, to trust Him, and then to act upon it. In so doing, I was untying God's hands and allowing Him to manifest His miracles.

I sought His will in prayer, read His Word, and sought counsel and confirmation from trusted pastors and Christian friends. It became clear: My priorities were out of God's will.

Knowing clearly in my spirit what to do, I resigned my banking job and took a part-time job without the pressure cooker atmosphere. The benefits proved unsurpassed. I now work in a delightful atmosphere for a Christian employer.

Incidentally, our family has never tasted of the "dry morsels." God has prospered us more abundantly than ever, and we are not only feasting on physical food, but that food is served in an atmosphere of love, peace, and security that only being in His will provides.

Father, place in my heart a desire to
continually search out Your perfect will for
my life, for I desire the joy and peace that
lies within it.
Amen.

Written on Their Hearts

Ruthi Cooper Neely

My son, keep my words and store up my commands within you. . . . write them on the tablet of your heart.
Proverbs 7:1,3, NIV

As our children are reaching their teen-aged years, we are faced with the age-old question, "Is there anything in the house to eat?" Every trip through the kitchen by two growing boys means at least a glance into the pantry to check the inventory. It's a full-time job for me just to keep food in the house.

While the food they need for their bodies is kept in the kitchen, the food they need for spiritual growth is found all over the house. I try to put it everywhere they might be, so that it will find its way into their hearts.

We have Bible verses in almost every room. Some are in cross-stitch, some are painted, and others are very simply lettered. As I have collected them through the years, my prayer

has been that these verses are being stored up in the hearts of my sons. I pray they will remember reading "Seek ye first . . ." when they turned on a light or "They that wait upon the Lord shall renew their strength" when they brushed their teeth.

This unusual decorating technique leads to some interesting comments. More than one person has asked me if I mind if they go around and "read your house." Our walls have become a silent witness to our guests and to the friends of our children.

A beautiful passage from Deuteronomy 9 tells us to write the commandments on the door frames of our houses and on our gates. It's a simple idea, but one with eternal significance.

Dear Father, help me to be concerned about the spiritual hunger of my family just as much as I try to meet their physical needs each day. Amen.

Am I Tearing Down My House?

Matilda Nordtvedt

Every wise woman buildeth her house: but the foolish plucketh it down with her hands.
Proverbs 14:1, KJV

I have always prided myself on being a good wife. Be unfaithful to my husband? I wouldn't even think of it! Neglect him? Not me! Even though our household has been reduced to just the two of us, I carefully prepare healthful, tasty meals every day. I keep his clothes washed and ironed, the house clean and neat. Oh, yes, I take good care of my husband.

Why then does the verse at the top of this page always give me a prick in my conscience and make me wonder if I am tearing down my house instead of building it? I have discovered that there is more than one way to tear down a marriage. Some do it in one fell swoop by asking for a divorce. Some of us do it in little bits and pieces.

"Honey, I put those paper towels in your bathroom so you can wipe the splashes off your mirror." (To myself: *Why doesn't he remember? I mention it all the time. It would just take a few seconds!*)

"Aren't you going to get into the right lane? We have to turn pretty soon, you know." (*Why doesn't he drive like I do—get in the correct lane miles ahead of time?*)

"Why are we taking this route to church today? Don't you think the other way is faster?" (*I know the other way is better.*)

Tearing down—one little piece at a time, disapproving, criticizing, nagging. "The contentions of a wife are a constant dripping" (Prov. 19:13, NASB). "It is better to live in a corner of the roof than in a house shared with a contentious woman" (Prov. 25:24, NASB).

Water, over a period of time, wears away even stone. What is my constant dripping doing to my marriage?

Lord, I thank You for my faithful husband. Help me to quit tearing down our marriage bit by bit. Teach me to build it up instead by positive, encouraging, and loving remarks. Amen.

Don't Take Yourself So Seriously

Nancy Pannell

A wise son hears his father's instruction.
Proverbs 13:1, RSV

Often, during those frenetic years of parenting, the counsel of an older minister friend helped my perspective [as the wife of a pastor].

"Remember," he once advised my husband, Zack, and me, "you can never take our Lord's work too seriously. But, be careful that you don't take yourselves too seriously." Sometimes, especially with children, not taking ourselves too seriously is the best response.

God has the most capricious ways of humbling us. Neither I nor some of the members at the First Baptist Church of Muskogee, Oklahoma, are likely to forget that particular Sunday morning—the morning I wore a wig to church. Remember the days of the fashion wigs? Remember how appalling one's real hair looked after being flattened under the wig?

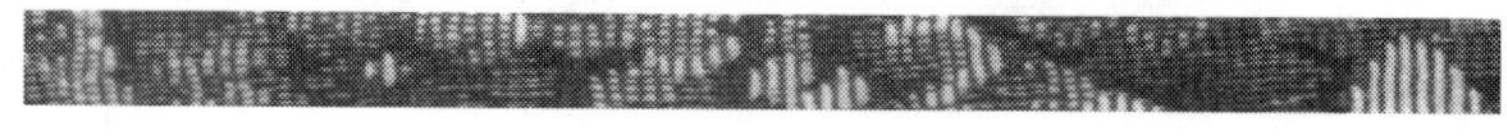

That infamous Sunday my daughter Carolyn persuaded me to sit in the balcony with her. To Carolyn, at age six, ultimate joy was sitting in the balcony right by the rail. That way, when we stood to sing or pray, she could lean over and look down and be both awed and scared by the height.

All went well until the closing prayer. I leaned over Carolyn to help her with her coat. (That's probably when God got the idea. He knew I was rushing to beat the crowd down the stairs, instead of listening to the prayer.) As I struggled with Carolyn's coat while juggling a purse and Bible, her arm shot upward through a coat sleeve, caught the edge of my wig and sent that wig sailing over the balcony rail, airborne like an unidentified flying varmint, to land unceremoniously on a startled worshiper.

In such a time, one has a choice—to weep, to destroy a kid, or to laugh. I laughed hysterically, like a demented woman, all the way home, after setting a new track record out of the church.

Curious thing about that incident. Moments before, I was feeling particularly impressed with my spirituality, with all I was doing to serve the Lord.

Lord, thank You for laughter and for the reminder that we should never take ourselves too seriously. Our work for You, however, is a very serious matter. Thank You for the privilege of serving You.
Amen.

Through a Child's Eyes

Frances Gregory Pasch

How blessed is the man who finds wisdom, and the man who gains understanding.
Proverbs 3:13, NASB

Many of our mistakes are evident immediately. Others take years to discover. Several months ago, a little girl helped uncover one of mine.

One day Nicole came to our house for dinner, bringing me a beautiful red rose and a box of scented bath cubes. She was excited about giving the gifts to me, and we enjoyed a special evening together. When Nicole left I placed the bath cubes in my linen closet and forgot about them. But she didn't forget.

A week later she asked if I had used them yet. I wanted to say yes, but I couldn't lie. Instead, I promised to start using the bath cubes the next day. That seemed to take away the sting of disappointment.

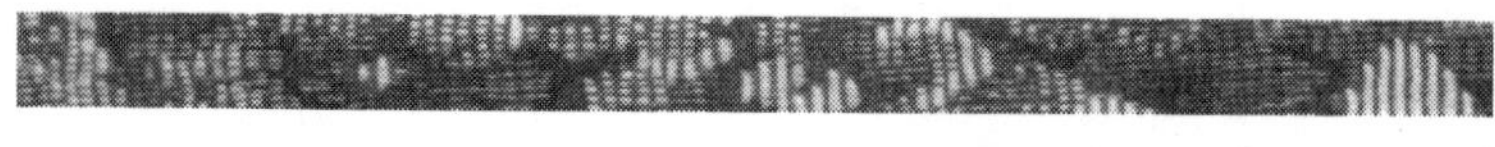

The following morning as I sat in my fragrant bath water, thoughts of long-forgotten experiences flooded my mind. I remembered times when my children were young and just as enthusiastic about the gifts they had made or bought for me. Yet often I must have disappointed them.

Back then I was always striving for perfection, and I worried about unimportant things. So when my children's gifts didn't blend with the decor, I just put them away and often never used them. I didn't consider the children's disappointment. I was more concerned with how things looked.

Recently while cleaning the attic, I found some of my children's projects buried in the rubble. I dusted them and displayed them, trying to recapture those precious, lost moments, but I was too late. The meaning was not the same for me or for them.

Then I thought, God has given us a gift, the greatest gift of all—His Son, Jesus Christ. Yet how often in the hustle and bustle of everyday activities do we forget Him too, burying Him in the attics of our minds.

But unlike the world, He offers us a second chance. He'll forget the past and wipe our slates clean. All He asks is that we put aside those things that have kept Him hidden and begin anew by making Him the center of our lives.

What greater gift can there be?

Lord, thank You for giving me a second chance. Help me to share the lessons I have learned with others, so that they, too, may have a second chance.
Amen.

A DIVINE PERSPECTIVE

Peg Rankin

Say to wisdom, "You are my sister," and call insight your intimate friend.
Proverbs 7:4, RSV

One evening as I was watching the national news on TV, I learned that Mother Teresa of Calcutta was ill. In 1979, I was reminded, she had received the Nobel Peace Prize for serving her fellowman. *What a ministry God has entrusted to her*, I thought.

It began on a street in India when she picked up one dying person. Today her Missionaries of Charity are caring for the destitute and dying in fifty-two countries around the world.

As graphic scenes of her compassionate outreach flashed on the screen, I became more taken than ever with this humble woman's dedication. *I have heard Christians question her theology*, I mused. *But I have never heard anybody criticize her service.*

Then I asked myself, *Would she have received the Nobel Peace Prize if her ministry had stayed small? Probably not.*

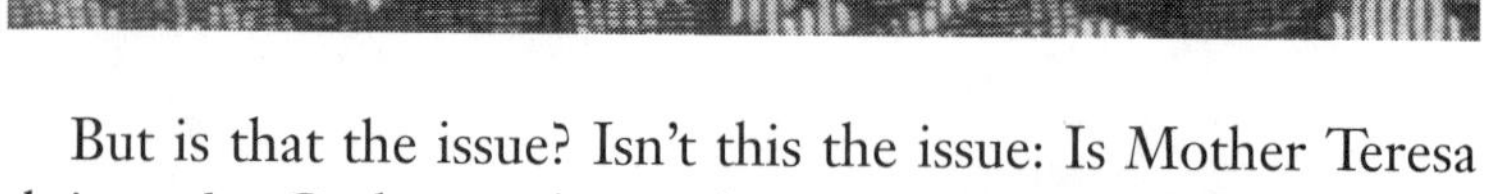

But is that the issue? Isn't this the issue: Is Mother Teresa doing *what* God wants her to do *where* He wants her to do it at this moment in her life?

Next I evaluated my own ministry. Not very impressive compared to Mother Teresa's. So for encouragement I turned to the parable of the talents in Matthew 25. As I read, I was introduced again to the three servants to whom the master entrusted money. One servant took his talent and buried it. He was rebuked when his master returned for an accounting.

The other two, though entrusted with unequal amounts, invested their gifts wisely; and in both cases their investments multiplied. Consequently, to both of them the master said, "You have been faithful with a few things; I will put you in charge of many things" (v. 21, NIV).

"Thank You, Lord!" I exclaimed as the light dawned. "The expansion or nonexpansion of my ministry is Your responsibility. My responsibility is faithfulness. Am I doing what You want me to do, where You want me to do it at this moment in my life? If I minister to thousands, fine. If I minister to hundreds, that's fine too. And if I give just one cup of water to only one lone soul, that too is significant. Now help me live this truth."

Dear Lord, thank You for the revelation
learned through the life of Your servant
Mother Teresa. Bless her, Lord, and help me
to remember that which is Your responsibility
in my life and that which is mine.
Amen.

THEY CALLED ME MRS. CLEAN

Deanie Remenak

Where no oxen are, the manger is clean, but much increase comes by the strength of the ox.
Proverbs 14:4, NASB

Fierce determination triumphed over weariness as I forced myself to scrub our kitchen floor again before I collapsed into bed. U.S. Navy orders had sent my husband out to sea for an eight-month deployment, so the only uninterrupted time I had to accomplish housework was after the children were in bed.

Cleanliness and orderliness had always been important to me, but studying bacteriology and microbiology had revealed the invisible world of organisms busily reproducing themselves into an enemy of aggression against good hygiene and a sanitary environment.

As a young bride, I armed myself with a veritable arsenal of cleaning products. I delighted in hanging out the whitest, brightest laundry. Our bathroom was immaculate; the kitchen, impeccable. Nothing escaped my rubber-gloved hands wielding cleaning cloths soaked in disinfectants, not even doorknobs and telephone receivers.

Newborn babies grew into crawlers, then toddlers. Each stage caused me to intensify my efforts. My children would be protected at all costs from bacteria, germs, and microbes.

Later, school-aged children brought friends home who had not been trained so strictly in avoiding messes. Even allowing for accidental spills and childish carelessness, my own children did not always adhere to my regimentation.

Love edged over closer to obligation and then to resentment. Couldn't they understand I was doing all this for their benefit? I would appreciate more cooperation. And gradually an overcommitted and overzealous mother showed definite signs of burnout. My convictions had turned into idolatry.

In His faithful, gentle way, my Lord brought my attention to Proverbs 14:4. Tucked in between two non-related verses was this strange agricultural homily about oxen and cleanliness. Then His still, small voice communicated to me the application of this truth. If I had no husband or children, my home would always be clean, but how many blessings and benefits I would miss. No hugs, no shouts of delight when freshly baked cookies came out of the oven, no enthusiastic greetings, "Mom, I'm home." Would I want to sacrifice all the love, affection, and caring bonds of a family for cleanliness? Not on your Lysol!

I will probably always want my home to be shipshape, but now my incentive is balanced and my idol has been toppled, crushed, swept up, and thrown out with the rest of the garbage.

Dear Jesus, help me remember how much increase comes by the strength of my family unit. Give me patience to overlook spots and stains as You in Your mercy overlook mine. Amen.

The Mystery Shopper

Sally J. Ritter

The eyes of the Lord *are everywhere, keeping watch on the wicked and the good.*
Proverbs 15:3, NIV

It was the end of a long day of substitute teaching. I had taught without lesson plans. The classroom was a confusing mess of books and papers. In addition, two new students had enrolled, which only added to the chaos. I had just turned out the lights when the principal approached me.

"Would you mind sweeping the room before you leave?" she asked.

Stumbling to the closet, I grabbed an old broom with a four-inch bristle span. "Only half a broom!" I sputtered as I counted the extra minutes this duty added to my already exhausting day. "Why me?"

Later that evening I was glancing through the newspaper. An item in the financial section caught my eye. A banking firm had sponsored a contest for its local branch employees to promote better customer service. Throughout the month each bank was visited by several "mystery shoppers" posing as cus-

tomers. Bank personnel were judged on how well they interacted with these individuals. Prizes were awarded to those people providing the most efficient, friendly service.

I thought about my own response earlier that afternoon. If that principal had been a "mystery shopper," I certainly would not have won the employee-of-the-month award. But then I realized that perhaps God does employ a cast of mystery shoppers. Had God strategically placed that principal in my life to bring about a desired response? The answer was yes. He was asking me to give my best in spite of the lack of props or appreciative audience. And I had neglected to offer service with a smile.

Since then, I have met God's mystery shoppers when I least expect it. The rude lady in front of me at the checkout line has been placed there to teach me patience. The young mother with the cranky toddler needs my words of encouragement. The weary Sunday School teacher welcomes my offer to teach her class.

When I think of every person I meet as a mystery shopper sent by God for a specific purpose, I am challenged to do my best. Am I a good representative of God's kingdom by the way I respond? Am I promoting His business? I know that my eternal reward is forthcoming, but God promises that "he who refreshes others will himself be refreshed" (Prov. 11:25). Lately I have discovered just how true that is.

Lord, help me to see the needs of people around me and then to respond in a way that will promote Your kingdom. Amen.

The Corrective Hand of the Vinedresser

Peggy Rogers

Young man, do not resent it when God chastens and corrects you, for his punishment is proof of his love. Just as a father punishes a son he delights in to make him better, so the LORD corrects you.
Proverbs 3:11–12, TLB

The morning sun streaked across my bedroom floor. This was the day I chose to do my gardening. I already had the end result of clean-up and pruning pictured in my mind.

Reflecting on childhood, I remembered Mother so diligently caring for her rose garden. I also recalled how meticulously Grandfather would measure and trim the hedges. Somehow, without even realizing it, I, too, had grown to take pleasure in gardening. I had great delight in cultivating the garden that the Master Gardener had provided.

One day I observed our city park gardeners trimming pyracantha bushes into shapes of animals. I was fascinated by the precise care and maintenance. This inspired me to give our landscape a unique look. I now had pyracantha trailing around our front windows, and today I was going to prune and train this beautiful red-berried plant to conform to my design.

As I began to cut here and trim there, my husband rushed over to stop what appeared to him to be mutilation. Of course he had no clue as to what I was doing and to the picture that danced in my head. I explained my vision, and after much convincing he left me to complete my mission.

Continuing to work, I meditated on how God desires to prune and shape me into the image of His Son, Jesus. I reflected on times past when I felt the pruning hand of the Master. Years ago, I would continually run to and fro to hear special men of God speak. Finally, God quieted me and directed me back to mediation and study of His Word. There were also times when I would become overburdened with ministry to others. God, then, gently showed me the neglect of my husband and children.

At first, God's corrective hand was uncomfortable, and I wasn't quite sure I wanted it in my life. But loving God and trusting His infinite wisdom, I came to understand His purpose. He desired fruitful growth. Finally, I was willing to submit.

God is the Vinedresser and we are the branches. He has the prerogative of trimming and pruning when He sees dead wood, pests, or insects. His correction and cutting away of hindrances shapes us into the likeness of Christ. Because He loves us, He corrects us. And He corrects us not as a judge, but rather as a loving Father.

Oh, Lord, help me to recognize and yield today to those things You desire to change and reshape in my life so I may be made into the likeness of Your dear Son, Jesus. Amen.

Laughter and Quiche Lorraine

Jane Rumph

The cheerful heart has a continual feast.
Proverbs 15:15, NIV

My worst home entertaining disaster took place the first year of our marriage. My husband and I had invited another young couple to come over for dinner, and I was eager to show off my domestic skills. After some deliberation, I chose a "foolproof" recipe for quiche Lorraine, which I had made successfully for previous meals.

Before the evening was over, I would prove the truth of this corollary of Murphy's Law: "It is impossible to make anything foolproof, because fools are so ingenious."

With everything else ready, I confidently finished preparing the green salad while the quiche baked in the oven. Then when Mark and Sue arrived, Dave and I welcomed our friends and chatted with them in the living room until the oven timer rang.

Checking on the dish, I was puzzled to discover that it hadn't set yet. I gave it more time and returned to the living

room, trying to appear nonchalant. On the next check, however, the quiche looked just as soupy as before.

"I can't understand why this quiche isn't firming up," I complained.

Sue, a mischievous teaser, joked, "Did you put in the eggs?"

"Eggs," I repeated blankly. Eggs! I had forgotten to add the eggs!

Mortified, I wanted to pull a bag over my head and hide in the broom closet. But the patient and forgiving laughter of Dave and the others soon calmed my panic. My dear husband reassured me that I had not lost his love, and then he rescued the meal by scooping out the mushy mess, beating in some eggs, and returning it to bake.

It's pretty hard to cook a quiche without eggs. And it's pretty hard to hold a marriage together without laughter. Thank God for the grace He gives us to laugh at our mistakes, forgive each other, and try again.

Gracious Lord, show me how to live life
lightheartedly, quick to forgive both
others and myself.
Amen.

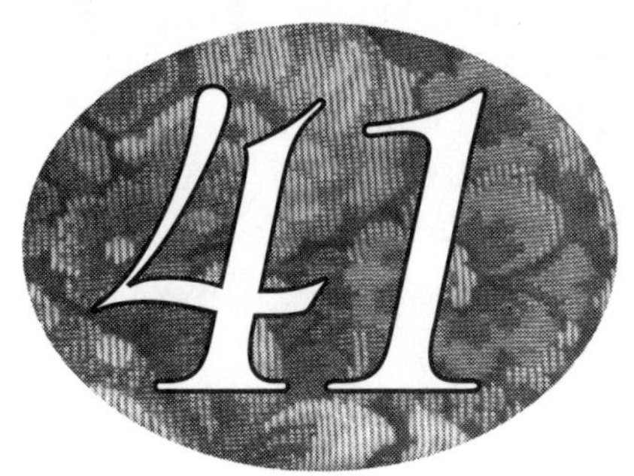

God's Perfect Number

Joyce E. Schmedel

A man's heart deviseth his way: but the
Lord directeth his steps.
Proverbs 16:9, KJV

Homeless! The thought brought indescribable panic. We had had no idea our house would sell so soon.

Earlier, my dad had died of cancer, leaving my invalid mother alone. She had refused to move close to us and would not permit live-in help.

"Okay, God, now what do we do?" In my mind I had juggled the principles of God's will: honoring my parents and meeting their needs, and meeting the needs of my husband and two children. Was there any way I could do both?

I rejoiced when my family agreed we needed to sell our home and move closer to my mother. It meant sacrifice for my daughter, a senior in high school, as well as my son in college. It meant a longer drive for my husband to work.

Our house sold in four days. Escrow was to close in a couple of weeks, but we had not found another house. In desperation we put bids on several houses, but to no avail. We were

confident we were in God's will, but where was God's provision and timing? Then the phone rang.

"Joyce, this is a neighbor of your mother. We heard you're looking for a house to buy. We had not thought to sell our home, but if the price is right we'll consider it."

It had only two bedrooms and a wet bar we didn't need. God's Word promised that whoever gave up a house for the Lord would receive manifold more in this life. This did not look like more to me.

Trusting that if this was God's will, our offer of a low purchase price would receive favor. Surprise! We were not only no longer homeless, but we could arrange a quick escrow. It would close simultaneously with the selling of our house. "What wonderful timing, Lord!"

Cramped into a smaller house, we made the family room double as a bedroom for our college-based son, home on weekends. The useless wet bar became bookshelves and a much-needed closet. The long drives to work became times of close relationship between my husband and my daughter, finishing her last months of high school. That in itself was a manifold of blessing worth the sacrifice.

Only later did I realize God gave us a house located on Christina Street with a house number seven, God's perfect number.

I praise You, Lord. You do everything well. You provide the perfect dwelling place on a street named after You, and all in Your flawless timing. We still reap the benefits of being in Your will. Thank You, Lord.

Amen.

Wrinkles or Smiles?

Debbie Schmid

A happy heart makes the face cheerful,
but heartache crushes the spirit.
Proverbs 15:13, NIV

Four-year-old Kylea enthusiastically skipped through the kitchen.

"Mommy, let's play hide-and-go-seek!"

"Not now," I replied. "Maybe later. Why don't you sit at the table and color a picture while I wash breakfast dishes?"

"Okay, Mommy," she agreed.

Fifteen minutes later her happy little voice said, "Mommy, will you play doll house with me?" I turned towards her while drying my hands on a dish towel.

"I would love to, but I'm terribly busy this morning. Can't you see," I continued, "Daddy's shirts need ironing?" I proceeded to set up the ironing board and started ironing. "It's a lovely day. Maybe you'd enjoy playing outside."

"Mommy, if it's a lovely day, can we go on a picnic? Please . . ." she begged.

Just then, the dryer buzzer interrupted. "Excuse me, honey," I brushed past her. "I need to fold that load of clothes before they wrinkle."

From the laundry room, I saw Kylea hesitantly open the patio door. "Go swing," I encouraged. "I'll watch you from the window. I love you."

I stood by the counter folding warm laundry when I noticed Kylea slowly trudging up the slight incline to her swing set. When she sat down to swing, her head hung low. With feelings of disappointment and rejection, her feet dangled in the dry, dusty dirt.

My heart sank! How could I allow dirty dishes and wrinkled clothing to gain priority over my daughter's deepest need for a friend? I immediately stopped folding laundry and turned the iron off. I quickly packed the picnic basket with her favorite lunch foods and called out the window, "Is anyone in the mood for a picnic?"

Kylea joyfully leaped off the swing and raced to meet me. Together we loaded our picnicking essentials into the van and drove to the local park. Her face beamed with delight as we shared our lunch with the ducks, climbed trees, and took a walk, hand in hand.

That night when I tucked Kylea into bed, she hugged me tight and said, "Thank you for the bestest day in the whole world! I love you, Mommy."

Dear Lord, please give me the ability to always recognize the needs of others and make my actions reflect my priorities. Amen.

The Small Coin

Mary Shamblin

Do not withhold good from those who deserve it, when it is in your power to act.
Proverbs 3:27, NIV

One afternoon the security guard at work came into my office announcing that he had lost the master keys to the building. Not only would this go against his record, but he would have to pay two thousand dollars to replace them.

As a Christian, I knew I couldn't turn my back on someone in need, so I stayed after work to help him look for the lost keys. We checked the whole building over, all the lunch rooms, up and down the hallways. We looked everywhere, yet there was no sign of them. Finally, very upset, the guard called for duplicate keys for the evening's work. My heart went out to him, and as we said good-bye, I prayed silently, asking God to reveal where the keys were. Than I thanked Him in advance for answering my prayer.

The next morning when I came to work, it was no great surprise to learn that the keys had been found. However, the way in which the Lord answered my prayer delighted me.

Late the previous night, the maintenance lady had been in the supervisor's office. As she reached into her pocket for some change to buy coffee, she dropped a dime, which rolled under a desk. Getting down on her knees, she reached way back to pick up the dime, and as she stood up she shoved the desk away from the wall. The missing keys, which had been lodged between the wall and the desk, fell to the floor.

As a result, the guard didn't have to pay for replacing the locks and keys after all, and his record remained clean. God had used a small coin to answer my prayer.

Lord, thank You for reminding me to go the extra mile, and for opening my eyes to see when You answer my prayers. And may I always remember to say thank You.
Amen.

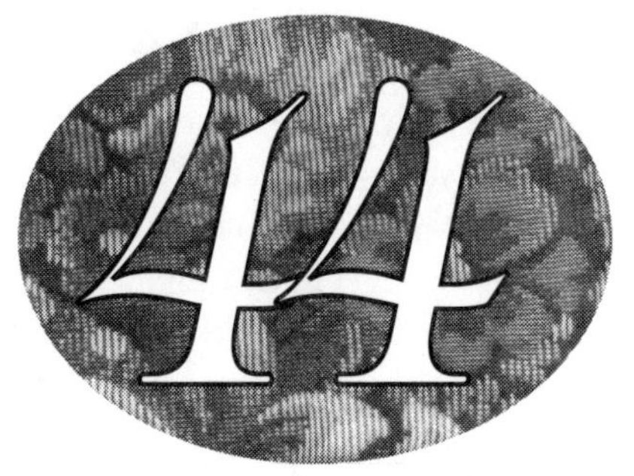

GENTLE WORDS

Catherine J. Svensson

A gentle answer turns away wrath,
but a harsh word stirs up anger.
Proverbs 15:1, NASB

Ed bristled with anger as he entered the Christian school office of our newly acquired facility. As the neighborhood postman, he had tried to deliver mail to us the day before, but no one had unlocked the gate, and he couldn't reach the office. That meant taking the mail back to the post office for next-day delivery. He told me in no uncertain terms that it was our responsibility to provide access for him on mail delivery days, or he would report us to the postmaster.

It would have been easy to match his words with angry ones of my own, but fortunately, the Spirit of God prompted me to apologize for our lack of knowledge and understanding of the situation. Ed wasn't expecting such a response and was speechless for a second or two. Then he began to converse in a normal, businesslike fashion.

We committed a few more minor infractions because of our ignorance of procedures. Each time, a member of our staff

spoke softly and pleasantly to Ed, assuring him that we would correct the situation.

Ed no longer came our way with a chip on his shoulder. Instead he used our school as a pit stop, using the restroom and getting a cool drink as he had done in the past when the facilities were occupied by a public school. He even had a special place where he kept his own coffee mug. And he helped himself to goodies in the teachers' rooms. As time went by, he was invited to fill a plate with food and join us when we had our monthly birthday luncheons.

At the beginning of each school year, we coordinated our calendars so that Ed knew the days when our doors would be locked, making mail delivery impossible. That way he avoided walking up the hill to no avail. We tried in every way to accommodate him.

Our staff made a friend, a staunch and loyal friend. And maybe that friendship will lead to his knowing and loving our Savior some day. It could have been the opposite. We might have waged a battle between ourselves and the postal service that could have gone on for years.

Dear Lord, may Your Holy Spirit remind us continually of the value in using kind and gentle answers in the face of anger and wrath.

Amen.

CHOICES

Ricki Teal

Charm is deceitful and beauty is vain, but a woman who fears the LORD, she shall be praised.

Proverbs 31:30, NASB

Tears filled Sarah's eyes as she searched for words to express pent-up feelings.

"I've lost the joy of living; my zest for life is gone. The children demand so much from me, and Jerry and I are growing apart. There's never enough money since the baby's costly illness. I have no marketable skills outside the home, and, besides, I can't leave the children."

I poured fresh coffee into our cups and agreed it was difficult to be a wife and mother in a changing world. Many young mothers experience the frustration Sarah was feeling.

While she felt unprepared for work in a technical marketplace, it was not true that Sarah did not have skills. Her dexterity with a needle was admired by all who knew her.

We talked at length about the important role of a wife and mother, and Sarah said she would live as economically as possible to remain at home with her children.

Later that evening our conversation came to mind as I watched a beautiful woman announcer give the evening news on TV. Outwardly she seemed perfect. Did she suffer from depression, worry about money, or sit through long nights with sick children? Was she more fulfilled than Sarah and me?

My Bible lay on the reading table beside my chair. I opened it to Proverbs 31. Long ago God had given us a description of a fulfilled woman. Her life revolved around the needs of her household, and yet she sold beautiful linens in the marketplace. An idea came to me, and I dialed Sarah's number.

Sharing my thoughts, I asked her to read the passage aloud. Moments later, excitement replaced depression as Sarah talked about the demand for handmade articles. Sarah's closets were full of colorful quilts and handmade clothes. Selling these items to shops near her home would provide needed income and encourage her artistic abilities.

After our conversation ended, I rejoiced that we have a loving Father who gives us guidelines in His Word and assists us in reaching beyond depression to show us a way to realize dreams previously undiscovered.

Father, thank You for being a gentle, loving God who fulfills our needs. Help us realize the importance of our influence in the home and teach us to choose what is best for our families and ourselves.

Amen.

Golden Words

Yvonne Unfreid

Like apples of gold in settings of silver is a word spoken in right circumstances.
Proverbs 25:11, NASB

I watched from my desk next to the large window in the school office as the usual hordes of children stormed the bus-loading area at dismissal time.

I scanned the crowds with a practiced eye. Classrooms had been warm that day. Tempers were short. Stored-up wiggles were finally being released. Fake karate kicks and chops fell harmlessly.

Then I spotted Danny swinging his book bag, daring others to get close. My spirits sagged. Only in the third grade, Danny was always in trouble. All attempts to discipline him were frustrated by his mother's intervention. I was not in the mood for a confrontation with the young man, nor his mother.

I continued to watch. Maybe nothing would happen. Then I heard a dull thud and a wail as Danny's loaded bag connected with another child's head. I sighed in resignation and headed outside.

"Come on, Danny," I called to him. "Wait in the office until your mother comes."

He turned to me with hate in his eyes. "You can't make me," he hissed. "My mom will get you."

Several nearby children gasped and stared at me as I struggled for control of my tears and my anger. I approached Danny, and he began to swing his book bag once again. I decided that I could not handle him alone and left to call the principal. "I'll be back," I promised.

On my way to the office, Kim, a bright, little red-haired second grader, who had been standing nearby, threw her arms around my waist. She looked up at me with her light-blue eyes. "I love you," she said.

I hugged her back and felt my anger and hurt draining away. "Kimmy," I said, "If you only knew how much I needed to hear that right now."

She smiled up at me. She did know. She was only seven years old, yet she had known exactly what to say and do.

I often think about that day and wonder if I am as sensitive to the needs of others as that little seven-year-old girl was to mine. Do I always notice the pain in a friend's eyes? A gentle squeeze, a hug, or a simple "I love you" speaks volumes.

Lord, help me to be more aware of the hurts of others. Make me a channel of Your lovingkindness.
Amen.

Forever Fashion

Clementine Walton

Strength and dignity are her clothing and her position is strong and secure; she rejoices over the future.
Proverbs 31:25, AMP

"Could I please dress up in your clothes?" whispered my little Navajo friend, Estelle.

I was delighted. After months of my working and living on the Arizona reservation, this child had finally gained enough trust in me to make this bold request. With shiny-eyed anticipation, she entered my large closet, dressed up in my clothes, and stepped forth looking like a beautiful young lady.

Now, a full year later, Estelle was back, whispering those same words. This time she brought two little friends who had learned about the wonders of my closet. What a picture they made, standing there with their long black hair, beautiful dark eyes, and eager brown faces. Estelle was the oldest and the most outgoing. Sophia was mischievous and pixie-like. Shy Geneva hung back, but came to copy her friends in this time of fun.

Within my closet was a paradise of dresses, shoes, purses, and belts. The girls were used to simple Navajo clothing, so a world

of adventure awaited them. They joyfully assembled my wardrobe into combinations to rival my imagination. In a chorus of exclamations, giggles, and squeals of delight, each girl made her choices.

"May I wear your shoes?" Estelle asked me.

"What about your jewels?" Sophia begged. "Can I wear the long pearls or the red sparkly necklace?"

Listening to their chatter, I thought about Estelle's original request. Doesn't the question, "Could I please dress up in your clothes?," represent a child's way of saying I admire you?

How I longed for these little girls to admire and desire my spiritual clothing much more than my physical dress. May they want a future in which they wear a garment of praise such as I wear. I pray that my dress of adoration for Jesus is beautiful to them. May these darling girls wear ornaments of grace and be clothed in strength and dignity.

Each of them dreams of a wholesome life, filled with the duties and pleasures of growing up and someday becoming a wife and mother. I want to have a part in that lovely maturing. But for now, I'll be content with the squeals and giggles of these little fashion plates, dressed in comical, yet wonderful, combinations, proudly parading forth from my closet.

Lord, beautify my spiritual garments by strengthening the gifts and skills You have placed in me. Allow me to model a joyful future for these girls as they grow in the likeness of You.

Amen.

A PROSPEROUS LIFE

Jaye Watson

But keep my commands in your heart,
for they will prolong your life many years
and bring you prosperity.
Proverbs 3:1–2, NIV

From the day of his conversion, my husband has lived in accordance with God's commands. He is not perfect, and I am grateful for that. His children will quickly recall many of his idiosyncrasies.

For instance, from childhood our kids have believed that any bathroom devoid of the Book of Proverbs (attached to the towel bar beside the throne) was naked. They joke about Proverbs suspended over their beds on a pulley that made it possible for them to greet the world each morning with wisdom "from above."

We added two little boys and a teen-aged girl to our family for a two-year period. Dinner time was special as nine of us surrounded the candle-lit table (candles help encourage good behavior) and read *Pilgrim's Progress* together "for dessert." Several months out of each year we retired the TV to the attic so that our lifestyle could be enjoyed without manipulation.

Discipline was established but seldom needed. Our children respected their dad. They knew he was in the Word and in prayer for them each morning. His slogan for himself was "No Bible, no breakfast."

Have we prospered? How do you define prosperity? Financially, we still live paycheck to paycheck. Our assets aren't notable. But we have the heritage of four sons who, with their families, love the Lord.

We have experienced some trials that in retrospect only drew us nearer to God and to each other. We can honestly say that it was good that we were afflicted.

We have blessing upon blessing. From youth pastor to elder to church carpenter and Christian dramatist, each son is serving God. All the wives are godly women who mesh beautifully with their spouses. Our grandchildren have many Christian models from whom to learn.

This may not be the world's definition of prosperity, but for me and my spouse, it's more than enough. The boundary lines have fallen for us in pleasant places.

Lord, thank You for our prosperous lives. Your commands are not burdensome and the rewards are so great.

Amen.

FAMILY FIRST

Mildred Wenger

Withhold not good from them to whom it is due, when it is in the power of thine hand to do it.
Proverbs 3:27, KJV

Yesterday my husband drove me to the city for a doctor's appointment. It was the eighty-fourth time he'd made the trip in the last year and a half. Because I'd had unexpected complications after surgery, I needed to go back many times for more work and tests. Each time my husband did the driving.

He knew that I would panic in heavy traffic and that I'm not good at parallel parking, so he always arranged his schedule so that he could take me. All in all, it was much easier for me when he was behind the steering wheel. His kindness in doing this for me is a beautiful example of Proverbs 3:27.

"Withhold not good from them to whom it is due, when it is in the power of thine hand to do it." This comforts me because it tells me there is value in doing all the ordinary tasks that have to be done in order to have a happy home.

When I was a young mother on the farm, I was very busy. I had neither the time nor the energy for many outside activities.

When I became tired and discouraged, I read this verse, and it cheered me.

Now that I am older, and more free, I am able to do a little volunteer work. While I enjoy this, I still feel my first obligation is at home. If one of my family members requires help that I am able to give, it is my duty to give it. My top priority is to fill the needs of those nearest to me, especially when it is in the power of my hand to do so.

Help me, Lord, to remember that even so
small an act as getting someone a drink
of water will not go unrewarded.
Amen.

Dirty Socks or a Destructive Attitude?

Betty Willems

Every wise woman builds her house, but the foolish pulls it down with her hands.

Proverbs 14:1, NKJV

There were his dirty socks again, lying on the bedroom floor. *There's no excuse for his carelessness and lack of consideration*, I fumed to myself, my face flushed with irritation. Angry words raced through my mind.

He would respond, "You're nagging at me again." And he would be right. But why should I have to do everything? Before hostility escaped my lips, the Spirit spoke to my heart, "Every wise woman builds her home, but the foolish pulls it down with her hands." Did I want to tear this marriage apart too?

The past flashed before me like a blazing headline trumpeting disaster. Suddenly I remembered times during the sad days of a broken heart, shattered dreams, and a divorce, that I had actually missed other dirty socks I frequently complained about. If only those dirty socks had been around when loneliness and despair overwhelmed me, I would have picked them

up gladly, and without a word. The Lord had given me a second chance at marriage, but reflecting on the failed one gave me a new perspective on dirty socks.

Gently the Spirit nudged my heart again, "Hold your tongue. Do not tear down this house by nagging and complaining. The Lord Jesus humbled Himself to wash the dirty feet of twelve squabbling friends. It is not too much for you to pick up your husband's dirty socks." Silently I reached for them and gently tossed them into the hamper. Peacefulness replaced hostility.

"I love you, honey," I said, without even a note of pity in my voice. Silently I thanked the Lord for showing me that love was more important than perfection. Was this God's way of teaching me what love really is? Yes, I decided. Picking up dirty socks is a little thing to do when it contributes to peace in my home.

Lord, teach me to cover criticism with love.
Let me not tear down my house with constant
complaints. Help me walk in the selfless love
that led You to wash the disciples' feet.
Amen.

My Children or a Clean Crib?

Karen Williams

Where no oxen are, the crib is clean: but much increase is by the strength of the ox.
Proverbs 14:4, KJV

During a Midwest winter's cold snap that had kept my six children housebound for days, I was bemoaning the state of my living room-turned department store. Canned goods and boxed items were lined up on the metal radiator covers. Books and copies of *National Geographics* had been pulled from the shelves for the pretend library. Pieces of paper were being cut up for book cards and getting tinier by the minute.

Clothing hastily pulled from drawers were heaped on the couch, with towels and washcloths precariously placed on the arms and back. Children's playing blocks were stacked on the floor, acting as room dividers. Stuffed animals in various stages of dress occupied every chair. Monopoly money had just been thrown into the air by an irate child customer who was told he couldn't buy food for his bears, because they weren't really his children anyway. My living and dining rooms were a conglomeration of my six children's personali-

ties freely being expressed. The rooms looked like a tossed salad!

Oh, Lord, I moaned. *How much longer can I endure a mess like this? Even when the temperature permits the children to play outside again, there will be the puddling of melting snow on my kitchen floor from six pairs of scattered boots. O Calgon, take me away!*

With Bible in hand, I headed for the bathroom, the one room in the house with a door that locked. O joy, O rapture! Entering and locking the door, I flung myself over the bathtub's edge. There, I wept away my accumulated frustrations and feelings of lack of accomplishment, fueled by the overwhelming endlessness of repetitious tasks. Doesn't anybody care?

When I had quieted from my outburst, I reached for my Bible, seeking comfort and encouragement. Turning to the Book of Proverbs, good for all weary mothers, I read, "Where no oxen are, the crib is clean."

As the Holy Spirit worked in me, I was able to once again repent and receive forgiveness. I yielded my desire to want a place for everything and everything in its place. If I had no children, my house would be spit and polish, but I want my children, and yes, Lord, the clutter that accompanies them.

Children have eternal value; houses and possessions are temporal and will soon pass away.

Father, please work in me the ability to see my children and the mundane things of life from Your perspective. Be Thou my portion again today.

Amen.

Words of Praise or Poison?

Lori Smithgall Witmer

Reckless words pierce like a sword,
but the tongue of the wise brings healing.
Proverbs 12:18, NIV

I excitedly anticipated the morning, which began with the best of intentions and plans. As a favor to my friend, I was going to baby-sit her daughter, Beth. This also would give my three-and-a-half-year-old son a chance to play with his best friend. As soon as Beth's mom closed the door behind her, however, the action began as if on cue.

Pandemonium struck with a potty-training accident. As I cleaned puddles and clothes, mischievous giggles erupted from my son's room. Upon investigation, I discovered them on the top bunk, slam-dunking toys into the fish tank below. Their aim was excellent. I couldn't see any fish for all their new accoutrements. As I fished out the toys and dried them, Beth and Eric ever so quietly exited the room. Following the sounds of laughter and squeaking box springs, I found them exercising trampoline skills on the master bed. In the process,

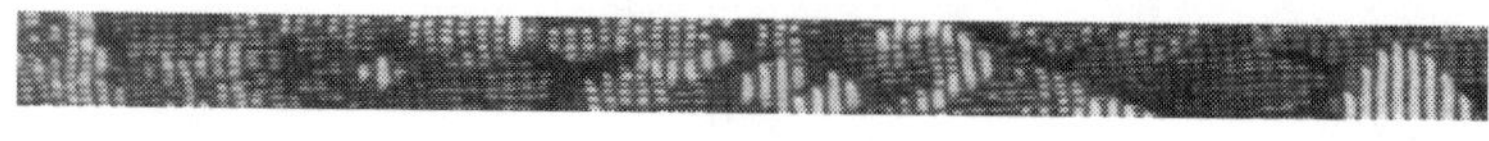

they had also awakened the baby who was sleeping in my room. Enough!

At wit's end when my husband arrived, I unleashed pent-up frustration from the past two hours. Although managing to control the volume, I told all, detail by detail, only to turn around and see the betrayed look in my small son's brown eyes. I had wrongly assumed he was out of earshot. He turned and walked away.

Days later, sitting in Sunday worship, my thoughts drifted to my curious son. Then a quiet prodding in my heart showed me: Eric needed to hear building words of praise, not destructive phrases of belittlement. My job was to look earnestly for praiseworthy accounts of his activities—to build him up by telling of his growth, rather than tear him down by recounting his shortcomings. This principle of praising one another was familiar and one we practiced often when speaking directly to one another. Yet now I learned my words carry impact, be it positive or negative, even when sharing with others.

Although it seems like a small thing, I am continually challenged. For even if the child is not present during conversation with others, the impression of who that child is as a person is being formulated. The question, therefore, is ever before me: With my words, am I building my house, or am I tearing it down?

Dear Lord, I am so grateful for Your speaking to my heart before I carelessly open my mouth and, once again, a little boy's heart and soul are injured. Continue to guide me in caring for and building up this most precious gift to me. Amen.

Soul-Winning for Jesus

Anita Wood

The fruit of the righteous is a tree of life, and he who wins souls is wise.
Proverbs 11:30, NIV

While shopping one day, I stopped at a styling salon to inquire about a job opening in another store in this chain of department stores. Believing I could find out about their salaries and what was required for a management position, I asked the woman in charge for information that would help me determine if I might be able to work for this company.

After explaining my years of experience to her, she said, "Please don't go to the other location; we need you here!" I committed to the job and began work almost immediately.

God gave me favor in this workplace. Within a year, I received several service awards; I was also given the nickname Preacher Lady. With that name came much ridicule, but the blessings that came by perseverance brought greater joy.

After a time, the girls in the shop stopped making fun of my faith and began asking for prayer. One young woman in particular needed special prayer, and I offered it up right at the

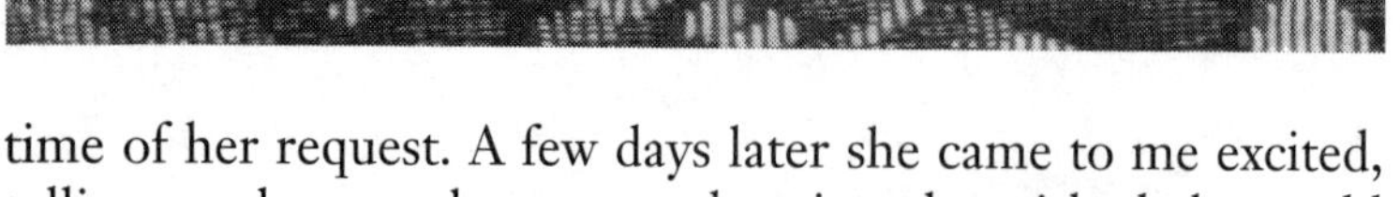

time of her request. A few days later she came to me excited, telling me her good report and saying she wished she could have my faith. I shared the gospel message with Amy, and in due time God gave the increase. Amy's soul was won to Christ.

I have found that no matter how things appear on the surface, if I press on and remain faithful, God will use my heart to see the lost come to eternal life. I have no special degrees or training in theology, but my Teacher, the Holy Spirit, gives me just the words I need, when I need them. My part is to reside in His Word and remain faithful to His call on my life, whether in my workplace or in my home.

Dear Father, as one who desires to be used by You, I come asking and trusting that You will help me to be a tree that produces life. Help me to die to self and let Jesus live through me at work and at home. I want to be wise. I want to see souls won for You. Amen.

HOME

Louise B. Wyly

Through skillful and godly Wisdom is a house [a life, a home, a family] built, and by understanding it is established [on a sound and good foundation].
Proverbs 24:3, AMP

When I hear the word *home*, I get excited and feel eager to arrive there. Why? Because my home is part of my personality. It's that place where my loved ones live. It's where my love and my creativity abound.

Home is where our family gathered daily around the table for food and fellowship and where blessings shared with guests overflowed. I can still see the scratches on the chair rungs, and I remember the little feet that made them.

I can still hear the happy voices gathered for Thanksgiving dinner. The smell of roast turkey and pumpkin pie permeates the air with love and thankful hearts.

Home is where my husband and I watched each little one take those precious first steps across the floor. It's where fingerprints were wiped clean from the walls, but not from my heart.

Home is where I've invested myself with fulfilled dreams and shared ideas, and it's where I was a partner to many plans.

Home is where photos of years of love never to be forgotten are displayed, where we can replay home movies on cold winter nights. It's where I shed tears for memories long past, for the nest that is now empty. It's where life shared to the fullest extent has left its mark. No wonder I feel tugs on my heart at the sound of the word *home*.

I feel a similar tug when I read John 14:2: "In My Father's house there are many dwelling places (homes). . . . For I am going away to prepare a place for you." That's my heavenly home, where I'll be with God for all eternity.

Yes, I still get goose bumps at the thought of home, but now, at this time in my life, the home that makes my heart beat in anticipation is my heavenly home, that place where someday I'll be with my loved ones, sharing life to the fullest, for all eternity.

Thank You, Lord, for homes. Thank You for loved ones. Thank You most of all for my eternal home where I will dwell with You and all of my loved ones forever. Amen.

Meet Our Contributors

Gloria Anderson is a retired school teacher who has published numerous articles, devotions, and poems. She enjoys being involved with her family, church, friends, community functions, and writing. Gloria and her husband have four grown children and six grandchildren and reside in East Wenatchee, Wash.

Linda Atterbury is an ophthalmic technician who enjoys singing, gardening, playing the recorder, and teaching drama to children. She and her husband, Phil, have three children and make their home in Santa Rosa, Calif.

Mary Jane Behm has written numerous articles, as well as a weekly newspaper column. She is a retired teacher, but keeps busy with church activities and writing. She enjoys reading, corresponding with friends and relatives, and crafts. Mary Jane and her husband, Harold, have three grown daughters and live in Charlotte, N.C.

Jan Boatwright is a Christian bookstore owner who enjoys art and writing, teaching Bible studies, and gardening. She has written several devotions, as well as personal experience articles, book reviews, and fictional pieces. Jan and her husband, Jim, have one daughter and make their home in Sandpoint, Idaho.

Elisabeth Buddington is a freelance writer of articles and devotions. She enjoys reading and music. Elisabeth and her husband have three grown children and five grandchildren and live in East Longmeadow, Mass.

Mary C. Busha is a freelance writer, the compiler of several devotional books, an instructor of writers' classes, and a speaker for women's groups. She also enjoys reading, traveling, and gardening. Mary has three grown children and two grandsons. She and her husband, Bob, live in Santa Rosa, Calif.

Suzanne P. Campbell has written over two hundred articles for publication. She is a rehabilitation counselor who enjoys traveling, reading, hosting foreign nationals, and, of course, writing. Sue has two grown children and resides in Minneapolis, Minn.

Rosemary Lemcool Capen is a freelance writer who enjoys sailing, snorkeling, traveling, camping, reading, sewing, and woodworking. She is married and has three grown children. The Capens make their home in Miami, Fla.

Lynn Casale is a full-time homemaker who enjoys reading, writing, gardening, singing, and cooking. She and her husband, Jeff, have two young daughters and make their home in Minnetonka, Minn.

Alicia Chai is a hair stylist by trade and a freelance writer. Her hobbies include showing horses, painting, and reading. In addition, she enjoys volunteering in the public schools. Alicia and her husband have four children and make their home in Harrisonville, Mo.

Pauline Ellis Cramer has written numerous devotions, children's stories, articles, and interviews. She enjoys gardening, weight-lifting and aerobics, sewing, cooking, reading, and hiking in the mountains. She and her husband have two grown children and one granddaughter. The Cramers live in Idaho Falls, Idaho.

Eugenie Daniels has written several articles and devotions. She is a homemaker who enjoys cooking, growing herbs, hiking, bird watching, and knitting. Eugenie and her husband, Daniel, make their home in Williamstown, Mass.

Kimberly De Jong is a homemaker and self-employed bookkeeper. She has written several articles and devotions and enjoys counted cross-stitch. She and her husband, Phil, have two children and live in Ripon, Calif.

Mary Jane Donaldson has written several articles, devotions, and plays for school children. She is retired from teaching and being a librarian and is now a homemaker and grandmother who enjoys clog dancing, swimming, and reading. The Donaldsons have five children and eight grandchildren and reside in Ventura, Calif.

June Eaton has published articles in more than fifty Christian publications for children and adults. A public school teacher for many years, she directed and instructed for Christian Writers Institute for seven years. June enjoys traveling and photography. The Eatons have three grown children and live in Villa Park, Ill.

Susan M. Ezard is a sales representative who enjoys camping, hiking, and counted cross-stitch. Her poetry and articles have been published in church literature and newsletters. Susan and her husband have two children and make their home in Lancaster, Pa.

Nancy Simmons Ferguson is a full-time wife and mom who writes "as often as I can." She says she has a passion for

gardening and struggles between her spade and computer. Her articles have appeared in a variety of publications. She is married and has three children. The Fergusons live in Winter Park, Fla.

Nita Walker Frazier is a former legal secretary who enjoys writing, sewing, and crocheting. She has written short stories, which have appeared in several magazines. Nancy makes her home in Plainview, Tex.

Linda Gilden is a coordinator of children's ministries who enjoys writing, reading, traveling, and attending sporting events with her family. She has written numerous articles and has been published in several magazines. Linda and her husband, John, have three children and reside in Spartanburg, S.C.

Carol Green is the author of several children's books including *My Mom Loves Me* (Cook), *ABC Fun Book, God Gave Me Five*, and *Color God's World Right* (Warner). She and her husband, Richard, have three grown children and make their home in Walnut Creek, Calif.

April Hamelink is a full-time homemaker who enjoys writing devotions, reading, sewing, collecting children's books, and working with children's ministries. She and her husband, Pete, have three children and reside in North Bonneville, Wash.

Normajean Hinders is a licensed marriage, family, and child therapist in private practice as well as an industrial consultant and conference speaker. Author of *Seasons of a Woman's Life* (Broadman & Holman), she enjoys cooking, writing, reading, hiking, and traveling. The Hinders have two grown children and make their home in Calif.

Marion R. Hocking is a retired school teacher and missionary who enjoys writing, reading, walking, biking, and jogging. Now a freelance writer, her articles have appeared in

several publications. She and her husband, Bill, have three grown children. The Hockings reside in Mesa, Ariz.

Jo Huddleston has written and published numerous articles and devotions. She is a former high school guidance counselor and teacher. Now a full-time homemaker, she enjoys reading, fishing, golfing, crocheting, and writing. Jo and her husband, Ray, have two grown children and reside in Auburn, Ala.

Judy Hyndman is a homemaker and part-time reading tutor. She has written several articles and devotions and enjoys photojournaling and reading. Recently her family traveled to New Zealand, her husband's homeland, where they were invited into the public schools to teach the Bible. The Hyndmans live in Los Olivos, Calif.

Rosalie B. Icenhower is a retired school principal and former newspaper reporter and writer for radio. Now a freelance writer, she enjoys painting and home decorating. Rosalie and her husband, Paul, have four grown children and make their home in Bothell, Wash.

Sharon Lessman enjoys reading, writing, playing piano, and acting and singing in community musicals. She is church parish assistant, organist, and pianist. She and her husband, Brian, have three children and make their home in Windsor, Colo.

Leslie McLeod is a full-time homemaker who enjoys sailing with her family, writing, singing, sewing, and gardening. She has written several articles, poems, and devotions. Leslie and her husband, Dan, have two young children and live in Camarillo, Calif.

Joyce Magnin-Moccero is a freelance writer and speaker and the author of *Linked to Someone in Pain* (Victor). Her hobbies include books, old movies, watching her children grow and learn, and being a Star Trek fan. Joyce and her husband,

Peter, have two daughters and make their home in Havertown, Pa.

Gina Halford Merritt is a home-schooling mom and freelance writer who has written short stories and articles. Gina enjoys being with her family, church, writing, and reading. She and her husband, Robert, have two children and reside in Ingleside, Ill.

Barbara A. Micek is coeditor and feature writer for her local newspaper, where she has received awards for her article writing. In addition she enjoys reading, listening to classical piano and Christian music, and studying the Bible. Barbara and her husband, Al, have four daughters and live in Fullerton, Neb.

Ruthi Cooper Neely is a homemaker who loves to read and paint. She has written several articles, and volunteers at her local crisis pregnancy center. Ruthi and her husband, Bob, have six children and reside in Spartanburg, S.C.

Matilda Nordtvedt is a homemaker and pastor's wife who has written several articles, columns, and short stories. She has twenty-seven books in publication. Missionaries to Japan for eight years, the Nordtvedts pastored in the Midwest and Washington state. They now reside in Lynnwood, Wash.

Nancy Pannell is a mom, grandmother, and minister's wife of over thirty-five years. A popular speaker at family and marriage enrichments retreats, she has written for numerous magazines and is the author of the book *Being a Minister's Wife and Being Yourself* (Broadman & Holman).

Frances Gregory Pasch has published numerous devotions and poems and delights in making her own Christmas and Easter cards. She leads two Christian writers' groups and enjoys encouraging new writers. Frances and her husband, Jim, have five grown sons and make their home in North Plainfield, N.J.

Peg Rankin is a popular speaker and Bible teacher who has led Christian women's conferences for thirty years. She is the author of several books including *Yet Will I Trust Him* (Regal) and *How to Care for the Whole World and Still Take Care of Yourself* (Broadman & Holman). She and her husband, Lee, reside in N.J.

Deanie Remenak is a homemaker and Bible Study Fellowship teaching leader. Besides writing, she enjoys quilting and sewing, reading, ministering to the elderly, gardening, and speaking to women's groups. She and her husband, Leo, have four grown children and seven grandchildren and live in Port Orchard, Wash.

Sally J. Ritter is an elementary school teacher who has written articles and devotions for a variety of publications. She enjoys reading, yard work, swimming, walking with her husband, and working with a newly formed writers' club for students. The Ritters have three children and live in Raleigh, N.C.

Peggy Rogers is a homemaker who enjoys writing, gardening, crafts, and water sports. She and her husband, Larry, have two grown children and make their home in Fountain Hill, Ariz.

Jane Rumph is a freelance writer and editor who has written dozens of devotions and articles for a variety of publications. She enjoys reading, needlework, baking, traveling, music, and volunteering at her church. She and her husband, Dave, live in Pasadena, Calif.

Joyce E. Schmedel has written several dramatizations and devotions and enjoys art, music, and Spanish. She is a homemaker and Bible teacher, leading several Bible studies a week. She and her husband, John, have two grown children and one granddaughter and make their home in Camarillo, Calif.

Debbie Schmid is a homemaker, writer, and speaker. Her hobbies include quilting, counted cross-stitch, sewing, home decorating, swimming, and bike riding. She has written several articles for publication, and an autobiography. Debbie and her husband, Tom, have one daughter and live in Tucson, Ariz.

Mary Shamblin enjoys writing, creating greeting cards, sewing, quilting, calligraphy, and other arts and crafts. She and her husband have three grown children and three grandchildren and make their home in Cerritos, Calif.

Catherine J. Svensson went to be with the Lord on May 10, 1993. Catherine had retired from Whittier Christian Schools where she served seventeen years as a teacher and secretary. Besides writing, she was also a speaker. She left behind her husband, Emil, and two children. She was from Chino Hills, Calif.

Ricki Teal is a homemaker and freelance writer who enjoys music and needlecrafts. Her writing has appeared in a variety of publications. Ricki and her husband have two grown daughters and four grandsons and make their home in Conroe, Tex.

Yvonne Unfreid is a retired school office manager and now freelance writer who also enjoys music. She and her husband, Richard, have two sons and two grandchildren and make their home in La Mirada, Calif.

Clementine Walton and her husband, Paul, serve as missionaries. In addition to writing, she enjoys teaching piano to Navajo and missionary children, cooking, reading, and sewing. The Waltons have five grown children and seven grandchildren and make their home in Kykotsmovi, Ariz.

Jaye Watson is a full-time homemaker who enjoys writing, reading, cooking, and walking. She and her husband, Bob, have four grown sons, twelve grandchildren, and one great-grandchild. The Watsons make their home in Mesa, Ariz.

Mildred Wenger is retired but stays active teaching piano, organ, and keyboard. She has published several articles and enjoys gospel music, attending concerts, and reading. Mildred and her husband, Daniel, have five grown children, eight grandchildren, and two foster grandchildren. The Wengers live in Stevens, Pa.

Betty Willems is retired from the retail trade and is now a Bible teacher and freelance writer. She has had several articles appear in a variety of publications. Betty is married to Jim and is the mother of four grown children and grandmother of eight. The Willems make their home in Post Falls, Idaho.

Karen Williams is a "household executive" who enjoys gardening, knitting, crocheting, sewing, playing piano, and being with people. She and her husband, Dick, have six grown children and four grandchildren and reside in Santa Rosa, Calif.

Lori Smithgall Witmer is a full-time wife, mom, and homemaker. In addition to volunteering in the public schools, Lori enjoys basket weaving, skiing with her family, crafts, and playing the flute and piano. She and her husband, Todd, have three children and live in Middlebury Center, Pa.

Anita Wood is the former director of Harvest House Shelter for homeless and abused women and children in Flint, Mich. She is a frequent speaker at churches and women's groups and enjoys traveling and journaling. Anita has four grown children and three grandchildren and lives in Liverpool, N.Y.

Louise B. Wyly is a freelance writer, part-time community college instructor, and library trustee. She has written four books for children, seventy-five articles, fifty devotions, and 150 Bible lessons. Louise has four grown children and nine grandchildren and makes her home in Minneapolis, Minn.

Credits

The following articles are used by permission of the publishers.

"A Wise Message from My Daughter" by Normajean Hinders was adapted from the book *Seasons of a Woman's Life* by Normajean Hinders, ©1994 by Normajean Hinders. Broadman & Holman Publishers, Nashville, TN. Used by permission.

"Don't Take Yourself So Seriously" by Nancy Pannell was adapted from the book *Being a Minister's Wife and Being Yourself* by Nancy Pannell, ©1993 Broadman Press. Broadman Press, Nashville, TN. Used by permission.

"A Divine Perspective" by Peg Rankin was adapted from the book *How to Take Care of the World and Still Take Care of Yourself* by Peg Rankin, ©1994 by Peg Rankin. Broadman & Holman Publishers, Nashville, TN. Used by permission.